C000277836

The
Southern Way

The regular volume for the Southern devotee

Kevin Robertson

Issue 33

www.crecy.co.uk

© 2016 Kevin Robertson

ISBN 978-1-909328-40-2

First published in 2016 by Noodle Books
an imprint of Crécy Publishing Ltd

All editorial submissions to:
The Southern Way (Kevin Robertson)
PO Box 279
Corhampton
Southampton SO32 3ZX
Tel: 01489 877880
editorial@thesouthernway.co.uk

All rights reserved. No part of this book may be reproduced or transmitted in any form or by any means electronic or mechanical, including photocopying, recording or by any information storage without permission from the Publisher in writing. All enquiries should be directed to the Publisher.

A CIP record for this book is available from the British Library

Publisher's note: Every effort has been made to identify and correctly attribute photographic credits. Any error that may have occurred is entirely unintentional.
In line with the new design the front cover image has changed from that originally advertised. All other information is unaffected.

Printed in Slovenia by GPS Group

Noodle Books is an imprint of
Crécy Publishing Limited
1a Ringway Trading Estate
Shadowmoss Road
Manchester M22 5LH

www.crecy.co.uk

Issue No 34 of THE SOUTHERN WAY
978-1-909328-48-8
available in April 2016 at £14.50
To receive your copy the moment it is released, order in advance from your usual supplier, or it can be sent post-free (UK) direct from the publisher:

Crécy Publishing Ltd

1a Ringway Trading Estate, Shadowmoss Road, Manchester M22 5LH

Tel 0161 499 0024

www.crecy.co.uk

enquiries@crecy.co.uk

Front Cover:
With two years to go before steam would start to be superseded on the Kent lines, an extremely dingy looking member of the 'Schools' class has steam to spare at Ramsgate in 1957. Underneath all that grime is a pristine layer of BR black or possibly even green either of which would have looked well against the crimson and cream of the coaching stock. *Norman Simmons*

Rear Cover:
LSWR bogie camping coach No 16, LCDR coach No 2 and one other arrive at Salisbury station on their way from Eastleigh Works to the West in May *1936. J. G. Griffiths*

Title page:
Isle of Wight Railway 2-4-0T No 13 *Ryde* was recorded by the Southern Railway official photographer probably around the time of its withdrawal in 1932. The location is not confirmed, but it could well be on the island itself – in which case a 'grand day out' for the photographer from Eastleigh (although he did have an amount of kit to lug around). No 13 dated from 1864, having been supplied by Messrs Beyer Peacock. Seven basically similar engines were acquired between 1864 and 1883, all named after island towns. Despite being from the first batch, No W13 (as it had been numbered by the Southern Railway) was the last in service and was selected for preservation, being moved to store in Eastleigh Paint Shop in 1932. Unfortunately this was not to be permanent and the engine was broken up in 1940. Note here that it is minus the front coupling.

Contents

This is the infamous 'signal' on the side of water tank at Eastleigh in January 1967. Not in any way connected with engine movements, it was merely part of the eyesight test undertaken by locomen at regular intervals. An inspector would take the driver to a specific spot, and a colleague would operate (or not) the signal, the driver being required to advise whether the indication was 'off', as here, or 'on'. Today this might well sound simplistic with, of course, a 50/50 chance of giving the correct answer, but it worked well enough for successive generations of railwaymen. The structure under the water tank had originally been a locomen's dormitory but was later used as offices. (According to Hawkins & Reeve in *Southern Sheds* published OPC, the shed offices at Eastleigh were destroyed by bombing in 1940 – des anyone have any more information as to where they were?) One other depot, Exmouth Junction, was known to have a signal for similar purposes, but were there any others?

Editorial

I spent a few days in hospital during the autumn – nothing major, just rather uncomfortable, as indeed most hospital procedures are. Returning home I was restricted to not being able to drive for a while and, after a very short time gazing rather aimlessly at daytime television, thoughts turned to being able to produce something rather more productive.

As this was a pre-planned admission I had previously set myself up with the modelling bench at the ready, an unmade kit laid out and (I thought) all tools and equipment to hand. Of course, once started I realised I did not have the necessary .45mm brass wire (not included in the kit), while additionally on just the second day I managed to break the one circular saw I possessed. Despite having said that I was 'prepared', I had no spares, so instead commenced a 'shopping list' ready for the next show I attended. Perhaps the main problem was not the lack of components or tools, but the habit that I know is shared by many of holding something close to my chest while working on it, only to find that said item falls to the floor – a dark blue carpet is not the easiest background on which to find a small piece of dropped brass. More to the point, a certain area of the anatomy was still smarting from having been poked and prodded and quickly took umbrage at what it considered to be inappropriate bodily contortions. Moral – a: take more care, b: next time choose a different hobby, c: in future have a different procedure.

While scrabbling around and looking behind where I had been working I espied a number of boxes of slides as well as notebooks and files that I will admit had never really been studied properly. This was part of a vast collection of colour slides taken by my good friend Roger Holmes. Some date back to just before the 1960s and, while the odd one has appeared previously in 'SW' I had never really found the time to go though the collection and sort out suitable images for future use. Now was that time, and I apologise wholeheartedly to Roger for his patience.

At this point I must also raise a general point over colour material that is already more than half a century old. Back in those days there was general competition in the market mainly from the likes of Kodak, Agfa and Ilford. None of us could have imagined the options we have nowadays, with digital and its generally forgiving software. The point is, should we even attempt to compare like for like over a distance of half a century, and how much 'adjustment' is acceptable today? If changes are made they should, I believe, be stated, otherwise corrections should be limited to a 'general clean-up', removing dust, hairs and the like. That is all we have done with Roger's images and I let the results speak for themselves. The important point to remember is a simple one: we cannot go back and recapture the same scene today.

Roger hailed from the east of Southampton and the fact that he is fortunately still with us today indicates that 50-plus years ago he was a young man who took railway images when he could, but was also required to work for a living while also having other interests. I certainly share one of the latter, being a dog-lover.

His slide collection was very much the contemporary scene, with many pictures taken around the Southampton area, but on occasions further afield, especially when he went on the various outings organised by the Railway Enthusiasts Club. In this issue we are delighted to present what will the first of many examples of his work, which we can also categorically state have never been seen in print before.

Moving on, it is a sad but inevitable fact that as the years pass so will those whom we had looked up to, and from whom we gleaned much information from the fruits of their own studies. It is with sadness then that I must mention the passing of Gordon Weddell, he of 'LSWR Coaches' fame. Gordon spent a lifetime researching, recording and collating the history of the rolling stock of the company, and his legacy is his four books on the subject. I know it is totally safe to say that his work in this field will never be surpassed. I had the privilege of meeting him on a number of occasions and he was the most amiable of people as well as always willing to assist with queries in his field of expertise. Gordon, we thank you and also miss you.

Kevin Robertson

Charles Anderson
From LBSCR to BR – Part 2
London (West)

To London (West) then, in 1925. My chief was Alfred Hooper Hoyle, who had arrived in London (West) from Exeter with the reputation of being a tartar. I was not Hoyle's choice and for eighteen months I had a pretty unhappy time. Little by little we came to understand each other and when I finally said goodbye to him in 1930 his voice broke. What a division London (West) was for events – Epsom, Ascot, Sandown Park, Hurst Park and Kempton Park races, the Boat Race, Twickenham, and an Agricultural Show or two for good measure. We once calculated that we had a major event on forty out of the fifty-two Saturdays.

It was at these events that I made my first acquaintance with the South Western relief signalmen, men who could turn their hands to anything – today a race meeting, tomorrow taking charge of a signal box they had never seen before and keeping the trains to time, next day relieving a parcel porter, the next assisting with a troop move, and so on. These men were giants in their way and there was nothing to touch them on either the Brighton or South Eastern. The traffic inspectors who had graduated from this school were the finest ever: Albert Payne, George Hall, John Gibbons, 'General' Gordon and Walter Case were some of the soundest railwaymen a company ever possessed. Dear old Walter Case could write a report on two closely written foolscap pages with one capital letter (at the beginning of the first page) and one full stop (at the end of the second)!

My acquaintance with the LSWR was of the slightest and I had much to learn. I spent a good many evenings in Norbiton signal box to master the working of the Sykes lock-and-block signalling instruments, which were arranged differently from the Brighton and South Eastern, only to discover that the LSWR had three ways of working Sykes, viz normal line blocked, normal line clear and, most surprising of all, normal line clear with signals 'off''. At Queens Road, for example, all the signalman did was to replace signals to danger behind trains. A train was offered forward before the 'clear' behind the last one, and the signalman hadn't a clue as to what train was in front of him. The LSWR signals and mechanical arrangements were good, but the company never understood the block system from first to last: all it did was to adapt the time interval system to block conditions.

THE
BOAT RACE
Saturday. 21st March
TICKETS TO VIEW RACE FROM BARNES BRIDGE
including Railway fare from WATERLOO to BARNES BRIDGE STATION and back now obtainable at the Booking Office (facing Platform 14) at Waterloo Station

PRICE **10/6**

SPECIAL FIRST-CLASS TRAINS for the holders of these tickets ONLY will leave Waterloo at 1.50 & 1.59 p.m.

Communications should be addressed to – Mr A G HILLS Booking Office Waterloo Station S.E.1. and cheques made payable to the Southern Railway

FREQUENT ELECTRIC TRAINS TO RIVERSIDE STATIONS FROM WATERLOO & SUBURBS.

SOUTHERN RAILWAY

Similarly the LSWR missed the train describer. These were generously provided on both the Brighton and South Eastern but there were only two very primitive installations on the whole of the LSWR, with the result that the code ringing on the block instruments from Wimbledon westward was unbelievably complicated as trains for the Epsom Line at Raynes Park, for the Kingston line at Malden, and from Through to Local lines at Marsh Lane all had to be picked out and coded differently. The headcode system for the electric

Sykes lock-and-block equipment in use within an unidentified signal box, but thought to be Knight Hill Sidings.

trains also had its vagaries. There was a 10-minute service of electric trains from Waterloo to Surbiton, alternate trains being projected to Hampton Court and Claygate (the temporary electric terminus). The Hampton Court trains carried the symbol 'H' but, owing to lack of stencils, the Claygate trains were coded 'H' with double dots over it. A passenger complained that waiting on Surbiton platform and wishing to go to Hampton Court he boarded a train carrying an 'H' but found himself instead at Claygate. He returned to Surbiton and, thinking he had made a mistake, was particularly careful to see that his train bore an 'H', only to find himself at Claygate once again! These, however, were minor points, and under Herbert Walker's efficient management the LSWR prospered.

It was, however, a long time before I got used to the Main and Windsor lines at Waterloo, which in some ways were poles apart; the term 'Up Main Local' seemed to me to be contradictory. There was still a preponderance of Drummond engines, a very heartening sight to the man who also served his apprenticeship on the Brighton where Dugald Drummond had been Stroudley's works manager.

What a pity it is that the best stories of Dugald Drummond, 'that cantankerous old Scotsman' as he was once described, cannot be told, at any rate in these pages. The following must therefore suffice. A driver put in a written suggestion for an improvement to Dugald's engines and soon found himself in Drummond's enormous room at Eastleigh. Dugald asked the driver to expand, so after saying that they were very good engines, he suggested they would be better still with a cylinder lubricator. Dugald got up and said gruffly, 'Take that chair!'

When the driver made some demur Dugald barked, 'Very well, then. I'll design them and you'll drive them. Get out!' But the old bear also had a human side, and when another driver was before him for some misdemeanour the man broke down completely and Dugald elicited from him that his wife had been sick and that he had had many a sleepless night nursing her back to health. Dugald pulled out two golden sovereigns from his pocket (a considerable sum in those days) and said, 'You're tired out, ma man. Go and take your wife for a holiday.'

One of the prettiest but highly unorthodox workings was that for Ascot races. The racecourse is on the up side of the line and all down trains went through a facing crossover (normally out of use) simply controlled by a hand-lever and plunger on the ground. At the west end of the station the train engine was replaced by an engine that had previously turned and the train regained the down line through the west crossover road, where it continued to Bracknell. At Bracknell, trains were run round, then proceeded to the up line where they were close marshalled for the return traffic.

In the General Strike of 1926 the London (West) Division had an unusually high number of men at work and I was lent to the London (East) Division, which sent me to the Brighton-side South Box at Victoria, where, with a very mixed team, we dealt with a minimum of seventy trains a day. Three incidents during this period stand out. The volunteer drivers had been treating the 1 in 63 drop into Victoria from Grosvenor Road Bridge with very great respect but one morning the Newhaven boat train came in with great élan and I was certain it was not going to stop – but it came to a stand in copy-book fashion. The driver was

Train describers at Cannon Street in BR days. Those nearest the camera are for down trains to Borough Market Junction, with the various route/destination options shown. This information was repeated on a 'receiving' instrument in the next signal box.

Another BR era image, but for comparison it shows the later (far less glamorous) replacement train describer cabinets at Victoria (Eastern). Operation now was by pressing the appropriate button, with up to three trains of identical description able to be described at the same time.

my old friend John Pelham Maitland, at that time shedmaster at Newhaven. My brother was not so fortunate. He was acting as mentor to a learner motorman who got overconfident with the air brake, causing the leading coach to mount the stops. My brother received a pretty severe shaking, but his pupil had the courage and grace to take the whole of the responsibility. The third case was that of a retired driver who fell into the old trap set by a set of straddle catch points. From his side of the engine he saw the open tongue and, thinking all was well, went ahead to become derailed all wheels.

To return to London (West), the lack of train describers on the LSWR has already been mentioned, and to overcome this single-needle telegraph instruments were provided between Vauxhall and Waterloo 'A' box. Three boys were employed round the clock at Vauxhall to describe each train as it passed to Waterloo 'A', where three more boys received the messages and passed them to the appropriate signalmen by word of mouth; but the fact remains that the boys could see the whole position much more clearly than the signalmen. I was pretty clear in my own mind that describers would not only save six boys but give the signalmen a much better picture. I had, of course, to win over the station master at Waterloo (who never understood the proposal first or last), but as his senior

assistant was on my side he agreed provided I did not take his three boys away! The station master at Vauxhall was fully in accord with the scheme and, as it so happened that the saving on his three boys justified the expenditure on describers, authority was given and the describers installed. Within a few days the signalmen could not understand how they ever got on without them. I then asked the station master at Waterloo for his three boys, but could only persuade him to give me two, but the fact remains that it has not often been the case that the saving actually effected was 66.66% over that claimed!

In the summer of 1926 certain Waterloo-Portsmouth trains on the busy Saturdays were routed via Epsom, Dorking and the Brighton line, and the LSWR drivers got the surprise of their lives at the easy Brighton route compared with the exacting SW route with the Witley and Buriton banks.

We had been receiving many complaints of the bad behaviour of passengers joining the Waterloo & City trains in the rush hours, and the Police Department wanted 30 shillings (£1 10s) per day to control the crowds. I offered to do it for nothing if I could have the services of six travelling ticket inspectors (men I knew well) for one week. I arranged for a stopping mark to be provided at the leading end of Waterloo platform and for white lines to be painted opposite the entrance to each car. The inspectors handled the job well and the passengers at once responded, so much so that I dispensed with two of the men on the Thursday and only had two the following Monday, after which we had no trouble.

In November 1926 the 5.40am passenger train from Waterloo to Bournemouth collided with the rear of a milk train between Farnborough and Fleet, blocking three of the four lines, while the breakdown train had to use the fourth. Passenger trains to and from London, Bournemouth and the West of England were diverted via the Mid-Hants line and I was told to do what I could to keep the freight trains moving. There were two or three up freight trains impounded at Basingstoke, so I telephoned my namesake (H. D. Anderson) on the Great Western and arranged for these trains to proceed via Bramley and Reading General to regain the SR at Reading Junction, leaving the accountants to fight the matter out afterwards. A day later one of the ancient trains on the Waterloo & City broke an axle in running and the technical people had the most difficult task as in the tunnel they could only get a lift of 5 inches. A few months later, the Underground held an exhibition of old rolling stock at South Kensington, and I pointed out to our people that the Underground was showing as a curiosity a much more modern coach than these venerable vehicles.

My job on the busy summer Saturdays at Waterloo was to equalise the loading between the various Bournemouth, West of England and Portsmouth trains. There was a very general dislike of the so-called Relief trains, which usually had no restaurant car, and which the public seemed to think would be put into a siding while the main train went past. If, however, you referred to the two trains as the first and second divisions of the 3.30pm to Bournemouth, it was quite different.

In August 1927 a new type of excursion was embarked upon with some hesitation – an excursion from Waterloo to Southampton Docks to inspect the RMS *Berengaria*. It was found a few days beforehand that the advance bookings were fairly good, so a second train was arranged. A third train was arranged the previous evening and the stock for a fourth earmarked should this be necessary. No fewer than 3,300 passengers turned up and a fifth train had to be found by taking an incoming train out of service and hoping for the best for its regular working.

There was a nasty little collision at Wimbledon with a District train in the autumn of 1927. The Underground road breakdown vans from Lillie Bridge were quickly on the scene and did some useful preparatory work with hydraulic jacks so that when the 40-ton crane from Nine Elms arrived the coaches were sitting pretty for lifting – an excellent example of a combined operation.

The excitement of the winter of 1927 was the blizzard. I spent Boxing Day morning at Waterloo cancelling arrangements for race meetings and Twickenham, and agreed with Roland ('Dicky') Richards (who was in charge, as Hoyle was on leave) that we should meet at the office at 6.00pm. It was not long before we learned that there was trouble west of Basingstoke, and Richards sent me there. On arrival I found that both up lines between Worting Junction and Basingstoke were out of use. 'Tony' Moore

had arrived previously together with a snow-plough mounted on an Adams 'Jubilee'. The only engines available to back up the 'Jubilee' were two Adams express engines, which with their large driving wheels were hardly the most suitable for the job. We turned the 'Jubilee' with its head towards London and coupled on the other two engines, proceeding to Worting with the intention of clearing the up through line, taking with us all the permanent way men we could muster.

On arrival at Worting Junction box we learned that an up milk train was in trouble between the Steventon and Wootton signal boxes. Not being sure that we could get through to Micheldever, we obtained a signalman's 'yellow' wrong line order from the signalman at Worting to enable us to come back on the same line if need be. We found the milk train at a stand between Steventon and Wootton with drifts forming round it. The permanent way men worked hard to shovel the snow away and we opened Wootton box in order to put the plough engines across to the up line. To enable these engines to go back on to the head of the milk train, a driver's 'green' wrong line order was needed from the driver of the milk train. The four engines started very gently but so great was the impedance of the snow that the train broke away. To join up the two portions, a guard's 'white' wrong line order was necessary. It proved impossible to shift the whole train so it was purposely uncoupled at the point of the previous breakaway and the front portion sent off to Basingstoke, the Guard going back to Micheldever to protect the rear portion. Single line working was then set up over the down line between Wootton and Micheldever, at which latter place the crossover points had to be disconnected as the weight of snow on the rods was too great to allow them to be operated from the box. More strength was obtained and the rear portion dug out when an engine was sent down from Basingstoke to Wootton and put across to the up line, but to get back on to the stranded vehicles a guard's 'pink' wrong line order was required – so we had used all four wrong line orders on one job.

I was recalled to London in the morning, wet through from the waist downwards through alternating between the deep show and the footplates of engines. On my arrival at Waterloo 'Dicky' Richards poured about half a bottle of whisky into me and telephoned my wife to have a hot bath ready so that I took no harm. For the rest of the week I took night duty, organising the relief arrangements for the following day. The West of England line was blocked near Overton but in our own Division the Mid-Hants line was impassable in several places, as was the Basingstoke & Alton Light Railway. I decided that the Basingstoke and Alton could wait and concentrated on the Mid-Hants, getting through three days later. A train was stranded on the Mid-Hants single line near Winchester Junction and the occupants of the neighbouring railwaymen's cottages fed and slept them until they could be got away. A week later to the day the thaw set in and we soon returned to normal.

Early in 1928 my old friend Basil Bushell (afterwards Assistant District Traffic Superintendent, London Central), Chief Inspector Greenstreet and I were appointed to codify the Block Regulations for the Southern Railway, and for good or evil those Regulations obtained well into BR days.

Kearnsey loop, Dover, is seen from a passing train. The train is travelling between Martin mill and Buckland Junction, while the branch to the right leads to Deal Junction.

In February 1928 a special train left Waterloo for a most unusual destination. It was the funeral train of Earl Haig en route to Scotland via the West London line, being hauled by Drummond 'M7' tank No 103 to Kensington Addison Road.

In the spring of the same year I had a most interesting experience on the Underground system. The Underground 'powers' suggested to the Southern 'powers' that an exchange of officers would be beneficial to both concerns. I was for the greater part of the time attached to 'Jimmy' Cooke, the Superintendent of the District line at Earls Court, who put me through the power circuit on multiple unit electric trains (which I soon mastered) and the control circuit (which I never did master). This knowledge was most useful as Herbert Jones, the Electrical Engineer of the Southern, regarded it as the closely guarded secret of his department. One of the first men I met was District Inspector Malcher at Acton Town, an old Brighton man who had known my father. He related how the Brighton Railway opened the Central London Railway, so he applied for a job on the new line and took with him another Brighton man to become signalmen at Shepherds Bush and Bank respectively.

Early in 1930 electrification to Brighton was to the fore and, as the preliminary survey had to be done in a hurry, I was detached from the Division for the task in company with another old Brighton friend, John Hercules Brown (later Assistant to the Chief Operating Superintendent), and very pleasant it was to walk the track in Sussex again.

The original Southern operating organisation was one of six divisions, viz Eastern at Dover, London (East) at London Bridge, Central at Brighton, London (West) at Waterloo, Southern at Southampton, and Western at Exeter, but on the retirement of Henri Alphonse Sire as Commercial Manager the opportunity was taken to merge Operating and Commercial Departments under Edwin Charles Cox as Traffic Manager, and to eliminate the rather unsatisfactory London (East) Division, which only extended as far as Epsom, Coulsdon, Orpington and Dartford. The new London (East) Division was to comprise in effect the old SECR, with Arthur White from Dover as Divisional Superintendent. This was a happy choice, as I think that Arthur White, a fine man and a fine railwayman, was the nearest to the ideal Divisional Superintendent I have ever found. Once again I had much to learn, but the historical background was most fascinating – the traditional battle ground of Edward Watkin and James Staats Forbes, who used their respective railways to work off their personal dislike of each other. It is not generally recognised that the SECR was simply a Managing Committee and that both the South Eastern and the London, Chatham & Dover railways survived until the grouping of the railways – as also, by the way, did the London & Greenwich, which was leased to the SER in perpetuity. The Chatham was in very low water, its ordinary stock standing at 24, having never really recovered from the financial stress of 1866, when under Act of Parliament it made an arrangement with its creditors; however, so loosely worded was the Act that a second one had to be passed to say what the first meant.

One of the oddest things I found was the fact that there was still in the company's possession quite a number of properties in the Hythe-Sandgate-Folkestone area, far away from the railway, which had been purchased by the SER in its struggle to keep the LCDR from pushing on from Ashford to Folkestone. At one time the SER acquired and operated an old toast-rack horse tramway between Hythe and Sandgate. This, of course, was miles away from any supervision and a colleague of mine used to describe the accountancy arrangements thus: 'Sixpence for me, sixpence for the company, sixpence for me, sixpence for the company, sixpence for me – oh, **** the company!'

What an interesting little line the Chatham was. The impress of Grandfather Sykes was still plain to see. It was signalled by Sykes lock-and-block throughout except for the Sheerness branch, which was Webb & Thompson Electric Train Staff. An excellent feature of the semaphore arms was that they bore the number of the corresponding signal box lever. The original LCDR ground signals were rather like a miniature smock windmill with a flap in front and a blue glass to indicate the normal position with a blue light. The lowering of the flap exposed the white light for the 'off' position. At one time there were in Dover Priory station ground signals of this Chatham type at one end and the SECR type at the other. The latter showed white for normal and green for clear, so within one station white gave diametrically opposite indications. In the London area, however, a most singular arrangement prevailed. What had originally been the block telegraph instruments were superimposed on the Sykes instruments and used for belling and coding. It was of course necessary for the signalmen to know the Morse code and trains were described by the telegraph call of the destination station, e.g. VA= Victoria, HV= Holborn Viaduct, MK = Margate, etc, so that the instruments were in effect describers with an unlimited number of descriptions.

Although a few Drummond unrebuilt 'T9s' had arrived, the engines in London (East) were South Eastern and SEC with only a few Chatham survivals – 0-6-0 and 0-4-4 tanks – while I saw the going of the last LCDR tender engine, an 0-6-0 goods. Two or three Brighton 'Gladstones' were living out their last days on through trains between Brighton and Hastings and on to Ashford.

One of the joys of London (East) was the little lines it touched, the Kent & East Sussex, the East Kent, the Kingsnorth, and the Romney, Hythe & Dymchurch. The Kent & East Sussex ran from nowhere to nowhere via the lovely town of Tenterden. Had it been extended to Maidstone as planned, it might have been more successful. The Loose Valley line from Tovil to Tovil Goods, with its elaborate girder viaduct over the river, was built as the Maidstone approach, but the intervening link was never completed. The locomotive stock in 1930 included Brighton 'Terriers', the eight-coupled tank *Hecate* (which was too heavy for the road and spent most of her life tallowed down in Rolvenden shed until exchanged with the Southern to finish up at Nine Elms), and an 'Ilfracombe Goods', to say nothing of a railmotor consisting of two Ford Model T cars back-to-back.

The East Kent was a sprawling collection of little branches serving various collieries. It left the old LCDR main line at Shepherds Well (a corruption of Siebertswold) and served mostly Tilmanstone Colliery and was continued over the SER line to Richborough Sidings, whence coal was despatched by water. The East Kent had a nasty little 'pitch in' and I was instructed by Gilbert Szlumper, the Assistant General Manager of the SR (and director of the East Kent), to conduct an enquiry. I was met at Shepherds Well by a special engine and saloon (the old LSW Royal Saloon) and proceeded to the site. It transpired that a coal train from Tilmanstone to Richborough was worked by a large 0-6-0 saddle tank acquired from the wartime Inland Waterways & Docks. This engine was too heavy to go over the bridge across the SER close to Richborough Castle, so the train was propelled to the bridge where the engine was detached and the train gravitated to the sidings – a regular working. On the date in question there was an important football match in the afternoon so the fireman, after dropping off to open the gates at an unattended level crossing approaching the bridge, did not rejoin the train to save stopping again. The guard was riding on the engine, so when the train was over the summit, he uncoupled and let the train gravitate forward into the sidings. Back went the engine to pick up the fireman and everyone was in time for the match. Unfortunately, a rake of wagons standing in the next road to that for which the points lay was standing foul and a terrific collision ensued, the noise being heard in Sandwich, a mile and a half distant, but not by the football enthusiasts!

Among the locomotive stock were two 'O' Class SECR 0-6-0 goods engines. To improve their appearance Holman Fred Stephens asked Maunsell to fit 'Whitstable' chimneys (the very stunted type fitted to engines working on the Whitstable branch in order to clear gauge in Tyler Hill Tunnel). This no doubt improved their appearance but it entirely spoiled their steaming capacity.

The Kingsnorth Railway ran from Lodge Hill, an Admiralty Depot, via Sharnall Street (where it connected with the Hundred of Hoo branch) to a jetty at Kingsnorth. It was part of a scheme for serving the fleet started by 'Jackie' Fisher, but was never brought to full fruition. It was purely a freight line powered by smart little green-painted 0-6-0 tank engines.

The Romney, Hythe & Dymchurch is too well-known to necessitate description here, but perhaps I may be permitted to remark that its title is as logical as London, Dover & Chatham would be!

Although it was not being operated in my time, there was also the light railway from Martin Mill to St Margarets, which had been used for the construction of the Admiralty harbour at Dover. Crossing this was the telpher line from Tilmanstone Colliery to the Eastern arm at Dover, which was to put the railway out of business, but British Railways is still there and the telpher line is derelict.

What a change London (East) was from London (West) with its events – in London (East) there were only two racecourses, Wye and Westenhanger – but the traffic density in the inner London area was intense and needed all one's attention. The showpiece in London (East) was the recently completed London Bridge colour-light signalling installation and I took many visitors over the box including French, German, Swiss, Swedish, Japanese and American, the latter frankly incredulous when we told him that we handled 2,200 trains per day. Soon after I arrived there was a terrific thunderstorm one afternoon. With recollections of what used to happen at Gunnersbury in London (West), I asked Control if we ever had any trouble with flooding. On being assured that this never happened I went back to my room but a few minutes later a rather shaken controller came along to say that we were in trouble between New Cross and St John's. The storm water had poured into the brick-faced cuttings on either side of the Lucas Street tunnels and the circuit breakers in the sub-station could not be kept in. Arthur White sent me to New Cross, but as none of the electric trains could move I could do little except, during temporary restorations of the current, get the electrics on the Local line and the steamers on the Through. But a colleague, not realising that the restorations were only temporary, altered the arrangements with disastrous results.

It may sound absurd but it is nonetheless the fact than we used to get troubles with an east wind. The down home signal at Dover Harbour was located in the Harbour tunnel, as the first points at the station were actually in the tunnel. The signal itself was a ground signal fixed on the tunnel wall. The tunnel runs approximately north-south and the smoke and steam usually cleared itself, but a strong east wind right off the North Sea would prevent the smoke from clearing and drivers, unable to locate the home signal in consequence, not infrequently passed it at danger. At Hastings, the tunnel between Warrior Square and Hastings runs almost east-west and is very wet, one track circuit being divided into several sections. Notwithstanding this, a keen easterly wind had an oxidising effect on the wet rail and we got track circuit failures.

It was during this period that I conducted one of the most extraordinary joint enquiries I have ever undertaken. A freight train left the down siding at Hoo Junction for Maidstone West, but although the signalman at Hoo Junction received the 'Train out of section' signal from Higham, the track circuit in connection with the Down Advanced Starting Signal failed to return to 'Track clear'. Having his suspicions, the signalman went out and looked at the down line to find a number of broken chairs. He arranged for the line to be inspected and telephoned ahead for the train to be examined. By this time the train had been shunted into a siding at Snodland, and when the sceptical driver looked round the train he found to his surprise that the fourth wagon from the engine was badly damaged. To cut a long story short, the wagon had travelled from Hoo Junction to Higham (about a mile and a half) off the road, breaking about a thousand chairs, had re-railed itself at the crossover at Higham, and then travelled on to Snodland. At one point between Hoo Junction and Higham the train passed an up train without incident, although the wheel marks of the derailed vehicle were 2ft 3in from the rail into the six-foot!

At the Joint Enquiry, the circumstances were reproduced as nearly as possible, and on the first test the wagon was seen to be rising on approaching the connection with the main line at Hoo Junction. On the second occasion the wagon rode right over the top of the rail and became derailed. The next down train was one for Sheerness, and if the Sheerness branch was put out of gear at midday it would be out for the rest of the day. There was nothing for it but to detach the engine and send it off to Strood, attach another one to the rear and draw the train back with the unlucky wagon off the road. We broke one or two point rods but the Signal Department men were handy and the Sheerness train passed with only a check. The derailment was due to a combination of circumstances – the supererelevation of the track did not run out consistently, while the wagon had unusually shallow flanges.

I soon made my acquaintance with what was probably the first marshalling yard in the country, viz Herne Hill Sorting Sidings. In the early days of railways freight trains were made up at the London goods stations, but James Staats Forbes explained that wagons would be loaded so quickly at Blackfriars that they would have to be sent to 'assorting sidings' at Herne Hill to be made up into trains. The sidings at Herne Hill had some wonderful names given them by the shunters. 'Bob' Pointer, a fine old Chatham man (the smaller lines breed railwaymen who have to be able to turn their hands to everything), and afterwards yard master at Bricklayers Arms, used to tell a story of a Board of Trade inspector conducting an enquiry at Herne Hill. The inspector asked the witness to describe the movement made, to which the reply was, 'Well, Sir, we goes up Teapot, down Coffee-pot and out through Ally Sloper...'

May we digress to some other (unofficial) siding names? At Clapham Yard the sidings might bear the official numbers 1 to 52, but to the men they are the Boathouse, the Contractors, the Lavender (from Lavender Hill), Beside the Fence, the Jim Brown, the Jim Brown Straight, the Up and Down Windsor (undoubtedly the former main lines), the Blue, Beside the Blue, and so on, winding up with the Post Office and the Piggery.

At Eastleigh the various yards are known as Tipton, the Field and Top End, while one siding is known as High Hat. At several places, be it whispered, there are sidings with highly improper names. Other examples that come to mind are the Jubilee, Ballarat, Klondyke, Spion Kop (these from the current events at the time they were laid in), the Garry (close to the Garibaldi Inn), the Rhubarb (next to the allotments), the Mazawattee, and so on.

Ask any Brighton or South Eastern driver the whereabouts of Nos 1 and 2 Up Reception sidings at Norwood Junction and he will look at you blankly, but mention the Teetotal Sidings and he knows at once. The reference is to their unfortunate distance from 'The Bird in Hand'. And a name the press can never assimilate is North Kent East Box – they usually 'correct' it to North East Kent...

In 1932 an unbelievable runaway took place. One evening a freight train was shunting at Addiscombe Road (Croydon) and some of the vehicles were left on the running line not properly secured and ran away towards Elmers End. It was confidently expected that they would come to a stand at New Beckenham, having negotiated the rising gradient where the line recovered

Paddock Wood looking east in 1932 with an unidentified 'Schools'.

Clock House station is seen looking in the up direction towards New Beckenham. The image was taken in 1946 – note the striping on the columns to assist in blackout conditions.

from passing under the Chatham main line – but not a bit of it. They ran on and the 'Vehicles running away on right line' code was passed forward from box to box and an electric train in front, warned of the danger, did its work at Ladywell in record time. The points were set for the spur to St John's where the sharp rising gradient ought to have brought the vehicles to rest in the station. The staff at St John's were ready to drop the brake handles as they passed the platform but the wagons were still travelling much too quickly, finally coming to a stand near Corbett's Lane – a runaway of something like 11 miles, but fortunately without serious consequences.

One unhappy feature of London (East) was the fact that in thirty months I conducted twenty-two enquiries into cases of fatal accidents to staff, usually the old story of familiarity with danger breeding contempt.

To be continued with a move to the 'Southern Division' at Southampton, and experiences during the Second World War.

SEE HOW S R THEY RUN

ON

SUNDAY, JULY 3rd

NEW TIME TABLES

will be brought into operation

including details of

NEW ELECTRIC SERVICES

—BETWEEN—

VICTORIA. LONDON BRIDGE. LITTLEHAMPTON. BOGNOR REGIS. CHICHESTER AND PORTSMOUTH.

DORKING NORTH AND HORSHAM.   THREE BRIDGES AND HORSHAM

BRIGHTON AND PORTSMOUTH.

COMPLETE TIME TABLE   -   -   Price 6d.

SUBURBAN TIME TABLE   -   -   Price 2d.

LONDON AND THE SOUTH COAST
via THREE BRIDGES

LONDON. PORTSMOUTH & ISLE OF WIGHT
via GUILDFORD

TIME TABLES

Price 2d.

obtainable at

BOOKSTALLS. BOOKING OFFICES. Etc.

Waterloo Station, S.E.1.
22nd June, 1938.

GILBERT S. SZLUMPER.
General Manager

SOUTHERN ELECTRIC

Hamble Oil Terminal, Netley

Photographs by Edward Pearce

There were definite advantages to being both a railwayman and an enthusiast at the same time. Being paid to indulge in one's interest might not seem ideal to all, but without exception those railwaymen who have over the years agreed to provide information to *Southern Way* have continued to enthuse about a career that to them was certainly far more than just 'a job'. Neither did it seem to matter much about the grade or role played in keeping the railway running. One such man was Edward Pearce, for many years 'in charge' at Netley, who fortunately took his camera with him on a number of occasions. Although to Edward the job might just have been the same thing each week, decades later it is certainly not the same, and we must also be grateful for his foresight in recording the everyday operation at nearby Hamble Siding ,which came under the jurisdiction of Netley. We may not have dates, but that hardly matters, for what we do have is a pictorial record of a once regular operation now fast receding into the distance.

The private siding to what was later the (Shell) British Petroleum distribution site at Hamble had opened in about 1918. Three reception/sorting/departure sidings were provided close to the junction with the main line, after which a standard-

From the vantage point of one of the lighting columns in the siding, looking east, the sidings are on the right with the main line and Hamble Halt on the left. (Hamble Halt opened in January 1942 primarily for the benefit of workers at the nearby aviation factory and is still in use today as simply 'Hamble'.) The road bridge carrying Hamble Lane over the railway will be noted; the twin arches are likely to be a throwback to early days and a consequence of a later doubling of the line. In the background is the northern extent of the airfield.

gauge single line of rails ran parallel to Hamble Lane (more recently the very busy B3397 road), before crossing the road from west to east via a level crossing and continuing at an angle of 45° across what was Hamble airfield. (A detailed history of the airfield will be found at two specific internet sites: http://www.hamblelocalhistory.hampshire.org.uk/Airfield.htm and http://www.hampshireairfields.co.uk/airfields/ham.html.

At the south end of the airfield was a loop, after which the railway again crossed the road by means of a level crossing to reach a larger set of loading sidings that included a single-road locomotive shed. Beyond the loading area the railway continued a short distance to a bitumen plant. The gradient on the line was especially severe in the vicinity of the loading sidings. Full details of the railway facilities will be found in the excellent *Handbook 'J': Industrial Railways of Central Southern England* compiled by Roger Hateley and published by the Industrial Railway Society.

Again from a high vantage point, the connection with the main line is apparent, as the railway curves towards Netley.

Below: '**Q1**' **No 33018** shunts the sidings. The brake van has been uncoupled and remains on the main line. For the purposes of these shunt manoeuvres a man was sent from Netley as required.

Tank cars await movement from the reception/sorting/departure sidings.

No 33018 within the sidings.

Tank cars within the sidings.

An example of an early wooden0solebar tank wagon still in use at Netley in the 1960s. Note that it is also unfitted and has simple three-link couplings. The label also refers to 'Netley LSW'.

Hudswell-Clarke 0-6-0 diesel-mechanical No 21 does some shunting. This machine was new in 1950 and, it is believed, remained on site until the rail facility was withdrawn in about 1985.

Below: **With work complete and the guard's van reattached, No 33018 departs with its train.**

More modern motive power in the form of D6508 (later No 33008) arrives at, works in and departs from the sidings. The number of closed vans indicates this was probably a general freight rather than a specific tank train; note also that upon leaving bitumen tanks are prominent.

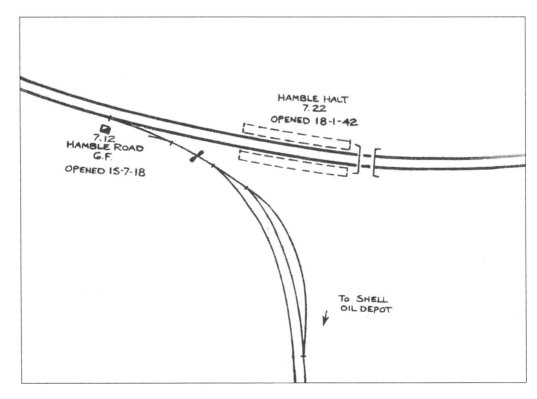

The main-line connection.
George Pryer

Cross-country cooperation

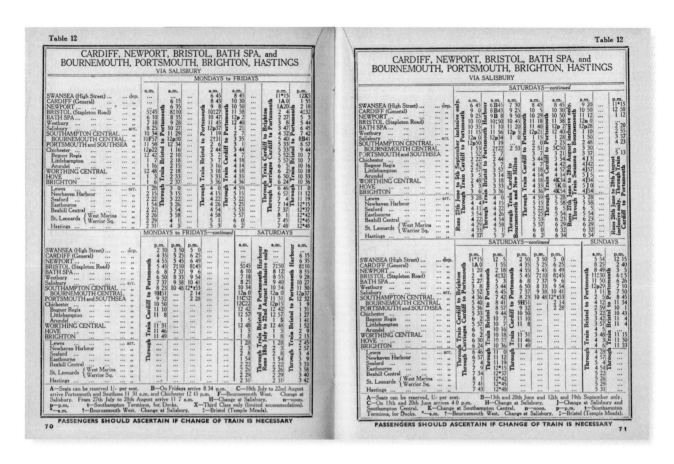

This extract from the 1953 Summer Timetable indicates an average journey time of between 4 and 6 hours between Portsmouth and Cardiff. (Best not to travel on the 6.25pm weekday departure from Cardiff, which did not arrive until 2.28am.) Comparisons with the present day are always dangerous, although it might be mentioned that in 2015 the journey time had been reduced to 3¼ hours.

Jeremy Clarke

Despite their warring history, the Great Western and the Southern – and indeed their predecessors – cooperated for many years in providing passenger services between Bristol and South Wales and the Hampshire Coast and Sussex Coast resorts. The Southern Region 1953 Summer Timetable No 80, for the period 8 June-20 September, and its Summary Table 12, illustrate this traffic well, although by this time the companies had both been subsumed into the nationalised undertaking. Demand for such services had picked up strongly after the deprivations of the Second World War and this was, of course, a time before the advent of cheap package holidays to the Continent began to make inroads into that demand.

As a rule, timings appear quite relaxed and it is possible that this is due, in part at least, to the backlog of maintenance, of the track particularly, because the primary cross-country route used could be described without aspersion as a secondary one. On the other hand the journey in the westerly direction, which is considered here, is generally against the engine for the 40 miles between Nursling and Warminster, if never extreme.

As traffic is largely seasonal, separate timetables in this edition appear for Weekdays, Saturdays and Sundays. Since Saturday is inevitably the busiest, workings in the up direction, of which there are a dozen, are discussed. Inevitably a number of these services run only at the high-season holiday peak.

The easternmost resort in Southern England to appear in the table is Hastings, all the principal points westward then being noted, with Brighton, Portsmouth, Southampton and Bournemouth highlighted. But the focal point is Salisbury, where engine changing would have taken place. Besides Salisbury, every train without exception calls at the main towns en route, Warminster, Westbury, Trowbridge and Bath.

The earliest train has not been counted as it would almost certainly have been simply a Western one as it starts from Salisbury at 7.25am. In common with all other workings it shows no connection from Waterloo. Neither does it feature in the summary Table 12. All stations to Bradford-on-Avon are served, then Freshford and Limpley Stoke before the call at Bath Spa at 9.08am. Termination is at Bristol Temple Meads at 9.26am.

Next comes a representative of a longstanding service, Portsmouth & Southsea to Bristol, running daily and departing at 7.29am. However, for those who could rise with the lark, a connecting train leaves Brighton at 5.10am, calling at almost all stations to Portsmouth & Southsea, where arrival is due at 6.39am, nicely in time for passengers to take an early breakfast before continuing. Connections are also noted into this train at Barnham from both Littlehampton and Bognor Regis. But a later daily train from Bognor, at 622 am and calling at all stations other than Warblington, arrives at Portsmouth & Southsea at 7.18am. For those on that part of what is now marketed as the West Coastway line, the extra 40 minutes in bed might be welcome.

So, we're away at 7.29am, but this also is a 'slow' train with calls at most stations before an arrival at Salisbury via Eastleigh and Romsey (so avoiding the tortuous path of the Netley line and potential congestion at Southampton Central). At Salisbury a connection out of the 8.11am from Southampton is made at 9.16am. A Bournemouth Central departure at 7.42 am, travelling via the now-closed line between Holes Bay Junction and Alderbury Junction, also connects at Salisbury. Engine-changing here takes a leisurely 18 minutes, then calls are made at all intermediate stations to effect a Westbury arrival at 10.32am.

Once more there appears to be no hurry to continue, departure not being until 10.56am, not that it matters much since the train favours all stations except Avoncliff Halt before arrival at Bath Spa at 11.42am. Bristol Temple Meads is the terminating point, at 12.05pm.

Thereafter a degree of urgency is apparent in the timetable. On Saturdays between 27 June and 29 August inclusive, the progress of the 9.00am from Bournemouth Central is, by comparison with its predecessor, positively meteoric. With an intermediate call only at Poole, it is into Salisbury at 10.19am. Engine-changing takes only 9 minutes (only?), after which, with the calls at Westbury and Trowbridge, the Bath Spa arrival is at 12.00 noon. Temple Meads is avoided by use of the direct line from North Somerset Junction to Lawrence Hill, to make Newport at 1.14pm. Cardiff General is reached 19 minutes later.

This train is followed by another 'Saturdays-only' working that runs for the duration of this Summer timetable. It starts at New Milton at 8.50am and calls at all stations before getting into Bournemouth Central at 9.12am. After a stand of just 3 minutes the train is away, favouring only Poole before a 10.36am arrival at Salisbury. There is then a wait of 14 minutes to make a connection with the 9.03am (SO) Portsmouth & Southsea to Plymouth Friary service, which arrives here at 10.42am. This train has provided advertised connections at Portsmouth from starting points as far away as Seaford.

Leaving Salisbury at 10.50am, Bradford-on-Avon is favoured in addition to Westbury and Trowbridge before a Bath Spa arrival at 12.14pm. Once again Bristol is avoided and, following calls at Newport and Cardiff General, the train terminates at Swansea (High Street) at 3.41pm. As some 1¾ hours have been needed to cover the 45¾ miles from Cardiff, it seems likely that intermediate places of importance such as Bridgend, Port Talbot and Neath would have been served. As this is a Southern timetable it disdains to enlighten travellers in that respect.

On Saturdays between 20 June and 29 August a train sets out from Fareham at 9.37am. Having called at Netley, Woolston and St Denys, it departs from Southampton Central at 10.09am, stopping then only at Romsey before a Salisbury arrival at 10.56am. This time engine-changing takes a bare 6 minutes before the train is away almost on the tail of the 8.50am from New Milton to make Bath Spa at 12.30pm. In this instance a call is made at Bristol, though the stop is at Stapleton Road rather than Temple Meads. Cardiff General forms the terminus, arrival being at 2.20pm after a call at Newport. A forward connection is advertised to Swansea, with a 3.53pm arrival there.

The first Portsmouth & Southsea-Cardiff daily train has connections noted onward from Hastings, where departure is another early one, at 6.08am, all but 3½ hours before the 'through' train sets out at 9.33am. (In circumstances like this one wonders, despite the inconvenience of changing trains, if it would have been quicker to go up to London from these East Sussex resorts and down from Paddington!) This train calls at Cosham, Fareham, Netley, Woolston and St Denys, getting into Southampton Central at 10.23am. Leaving 2 minutes later, a stop is made at Romsey before arrival at Salisbury at 11.05am; departure thence is 10 minutes later. This train also favours Bradford-on-Avon and makes it into Bath Spa at 12.43pm. Following calls at Stapleton Road and Newport, arrival at Cardiff is only 5 minutes after the train from Fareham. As with that one, the advertised connection to Swansea provides a 3.53pm arrival.

A second 'through' Portsmouth-Cardiff daily working departs at 10.34am, though its Saturday timings vary from the weekday ones. Connections are again shown from Hastings onwards, but with the instruction that those are made at Southampton Central rather than Portsmouth itself. This Cardiff working adds Fratton to the usual calls to Southampton, where departure is at 11.30am after a scheduled stop of only 1 minute. On Saturdays between 18 July and 22 August – at this time August Bank Holiday was on the first Monday of the month and not the last as it is now, which may account for the final date – Dunbridge and Dean as well as Romsey both receive the train's attention, Salisbury being reached at 12.20pm. Six minutes suffice for engine changing and the train is into Bath Spa at 1.56pm, termination at Cardiff General being at 3.45pm after Stapleton Road and Newport have seen it. On weekdays as well as on Saturdays, other than those noted the train runs all-stations between Salisbury and Bath Spa and terminates at Temple Meads at 3.03pm; no onward connections are shown (shewn?).

A 9.47am departure from Brighton provides a connection into the 11.15am from Portsmouth to Bristol. This train, again restricted to Saturdays between 18 July and 22 August, stops only at Fareham before a Southampton call between 12.03 and 12.07pm. After serving Romsey, the Salisbury arrival is timed at 12.48pm. Five minutes later the train takes up its weekday path as a 'stopper', getting into Bristol TM at 3.03pm.

With a plethora of 1950s and 1960s images of the through workings in the Roger Holmes colour section later in this issue, we have restricted ourselves to three pre-war images of through trains in the Portsmouth area, believed to date from about 1937. The first of these shows a Drummond 4-4-0 at Fratton station waiting to depart north with GWR stock. While Roger Holmes's views depict a predominance of Southern stock on the through workings, these pre-war views indicate that it was GWR stock that was seen, although this might of course be a coincidence. *D. Hammersley collection*

The succession continues with the daily 11.37am from Portsmouth Harbour to Cardiff, the first on which it is advertised that seats may be reserved. In the summary Table 12, this train, uniquely, has no connections at all marked from the east on a Saturday, yet the fuller Table 73 shows a Brighton departure at 10.17am, which will make it. Peculiar. The Saturday timing is another at variance with the Monday-Friday working.

The train makes a call only at Fareham between Portsmouth & Southsea and Southampton Central, where there is a noted connection from Bournemouth by use of the 'through' York/Newcastle train leaving Central at 11.16am. Departure from Southampton is at 12.37pm after a 2-minute call, before the train, unusually, then runs non-stop to Salisbury in 40 minutes. After a 1.25pm departure and with the two usual calls, the train gets into Bath Spa at 2.44pm. As before, Stapleton Road and Newport both see it before arrival at Cardiff General at 4.25pm. (The Monday-Friday working is 27 minutes slower.)

Another daily train follows, at 11.00am from Brighton, reserving seats again being possible from here and Worthing Central. Connections are provided from the east by the 9.15am from Hastings. Following calls at Worthing Central, Barnham, Chichester and Fareham – Portsmouth is avoided by use of the Farlington Junction-Cosham Junction spur – arrival at Southampton Central is at 12.45pm. The 2-minute stop here seems to be barely enough to top up the tender for the onward non-stop run to Salisbury, where arrival is timed at 1.31pm. Departure occurs 19 minutes later and, after the usual call at Warminster, the train is into Westbury at 2.34pm.

Bradford-on-Avon is added to the Trowbridge stop before a Bath Spa arrival at 3.20pm. Calls at Stapleton Road and Newport follow and Cardiff General is reached at 4.52pm.

There is a short lull now before the afternoon Portsmouth & Southsea-Bristol working leaves at 2.33pm. Comprehensive connections are shown into this at all points westwards from Hastings (departure at 9.15 am!). Fratton is the only station favoured before Southampton Central, but a stopping service leaving Portsmouth half an hour earlier provides a 10-minute connection at Southampton. Departure is at 3.20pm and, as well as the usual Romsey stop, calls are made at Dunbridge and Dean before a Salisbury arrival at 4.08pm. There is a footnote in the Summary Table 12 that advises passengers for Newport, Cardiff General and Swansea High Street to take the 5.02pm departure from Salisbury and change at Westbury. This may seem odd when this train itself makes a call at Westbury. Perhaps the timetablers, being Southern-orientated, knew what Salisbury station and City had to offer during the wait whereas Westbury was 'foreign' and therefore unknown territory.

In any event Salisbury is left at 4.18 pm with calls at every station from Warminster onwards other than Avoncliff Halt before arrival at Bath Spa at 5.29pm. Temple Meads is reached 28 minutes later. Whether any stops are made intermediately is not shown. They, after all, were in the Western's domain!

A Saturdays-only train follows, though it runs for a rather longer period than those that precede it, 27 June to 5 September inclusive. Departure from Portsmouth & Southsea is at 3.03pm, reserving seats being possible. A connecting

Again a Southern engine and GWR stock, as an unidentified 'Mogul' awaits departure from Portsmouth & Southsea. *D. Hammersley collection*

service has set out from Hastings at 12.15pm, though as with other similar workings it is probable a change is required at Brighton. (The layout there was and remains restricted, only one platform permitting direct transfer between the west and east, and even now for a train no more than four coaches long.) The 2.48pm service from Bournemouth Central is advertised as making the connection at Southampton, being the 1.25pm (SO) Weymouth-Waterloo. However, for passengers off this there is a 36-minute wait before departure for Wales at 4.00pm. After making the Romsey call the train is into Salisbury at 4.45pm. Not for first time in the table, onward connections to Exeter Central and Plymouth Friary are noted.

The stop is of 17 minutes duration and other than the usual 'miss' at Avoncliff Halt all stations are served before a 7.07pm arrival at Bath Spa. Cardiff General sees the train arrive at 8.47pm following calls at Stapleton Road and Newport.

Obviously anticipating a rundown in demand as the day progresses, toward its conclusion there are long gaps until and between the penultimate and final westbound movements. Portsmouth & Southsea sees the next train, another for Cardiff, leave at 5.45pm. As before, connections are shown from as far away as Hastings, in this case with a 2.45pm departure, though apparently also requiring a change at Brighton. This again begs the question as to whether it would be quicker to go into London and out again. Be that as it may, Fratton, Cosham, Fareham, Netley, Woolston and St Denys receive the train before arrival at Southampton Central at 6.41pm. The 5.16pm connection from Bournemouth is in the form of a Waterloo train leaving the West station at 5.05pm. The generous 11 minutes timetabled to cover the departures between stations 1½ miles apart is because, Saturdays excepted, the train is joined at Central by an up Weymouth portion, having left there at 3.50pm. Having called at almost all stations to Brockenhurst,

the train is then fast to Southampton, arriving at 6.16pm and so providing another lengthy wait of 28 minutes before 6.44pm departure of the train from Portsmouth.

After the usual call at Romsey, Salisbury is reached by 7.25pm. There are noted connections here to Exeter Central and Plymouth Friary, the latter reached at 12.12am on Sunday, but 2 minutes earlier on the other six days of the week. Ten minutes are spent at Salisbury, Westbury seeing the train at 8.20pm. Departure is 4 minutes later and, following the Trowbridge call, arrival at Bath Spa is at 8.56pm. As usual Stapleton Road and Newport are served before termination at Cardiff General at 10.40pm.

The whole evening passes before the final Portsmouth departure, at 11.16pm. As before, connecting timings are shown from Hastings. But tracing the progress of this last train across country provides something of a puzzle. The Summary Timetable 12 shows timings right through to Swansea, though most of these are obviously early on Sunday morning. And Swansea itself is actually reached post-meridiem, 13 hours after leaving Portsmouth. However, Table 80 (Salisbury, Westbury, Trowbridge and Bath Spa) makes no mention of this train, while Table 73 (Portsmouth, Gosport, Fareham, Southampton, Andover, Salisbury and Westbury) shows it terminating at Eastleigh at 12.07am on Sunday. Hmm, odd.

Well, a call is supposedly made at Southampton at 1.10am, but it is hardly likely that the train would take all but 2 hours to cover the 25 miles from Portsmouth. Bournemouth also gets in on the act with a departure from Central noted at 11.30pm. But Table 48 (Bournemouth, Salisbury and Brockenhurst) proves equally unhelpful. Table 12 shows departure from Salisbury at 2.55am. So, is Table 50 (Waterloo to the West of England) any more helpful? Well, at first glance, no. There's a 2.48am departure shown there, but that's slow

Possibly the most interesting of the three photographs, what is clearly a GWR '43xx'/'53xx' series 'Mogul' enters Fratton on the last leg of the journey to Portsmouth. The stock is GWR, but just look at that first vehicle – four-wheel LSWR without a doubt. The presence of the GWR loco also raises questions. We know that in the 1950s Salisbury was where engines were usually changed on these services, larger engines from both of what were then the regions being used – Bulleid 'Pacifics' for the SR and 'Castle', 'Hall' and 'County' classes from the WR. Before the war we may assume it was of the type seen, but why the presence of the GWR engine here on the Southern – extra working or engine failure? *D. Hammersley collection*

down the main line to Yeovil Town. Hey, but hang on. A note at the foot of that column states that this is the 1.55am from Eastleigh. Back to Table 73 and there it is, the first entry in the Sunday column, 1.55am to Salisbury, arrive 2.36am. And right next to it the 2.55am 'Through Train to Bristol, (Table 80)', arriving at Westbury at 3.35am! So back to Table 80 and there it is again, bold as brass in the first Sunday column with a little notation squeezed alongside the first few entries, 'Sat.ngts'. Odd that Table 12 includes the entire train in the Saturday table with symbols signifying 'am' against the later times, but Table 80 puts the service complete into the Sunday section. Perhaps the timetable people decided to have a bit of fun with it. Anyway, problem solved.

There's no departure time at Westbury as the stop is to 'set down only', though Trowbridge has no such restriction. With a 3.48am departure and a non-stop run thence to Bath Spa in 22 minutes, the train is into Temple Meads at 4.39am.

So, let's go back to see if we can deduce how the Bournemouth and Southampton connections are made. The pointers are all there now that Eastleigh has been established as the centre of attention. Table 45 supplies the answer in the form of the last up train from Weymouth, at 9.55pm on Saturday evening. This stops at all stations to Bournemouth Central, arriving at 11.25pm. With an 11.30pm departure and calls at Christchurch, New Milton, Sway and Brockenhurst, it reaches Southampton Central at 12.26am on Sunday. Eleven minutes later it is into the Terminus station, leaving there after reversal at 1.10am for the 10-minute run to Eastleigh.

Looking at these timings objectively one rather hopes that the Eastleigh Refreshment Room was still in business at that time on a Sunday morning, particularly as passengers from Portsmouth have 108 minutes to wait between trains. The 35 minutes facing those off the up Waterloo train from Weymouth/Bournemouth could also seem interminable at that time of night, even in high summer.

So how does the service compare to that of today? That for summer 2015 provides quite a contrast, though significantly no connections are shown from points east of Brighton or west of Cardiff. First Great Western dominates the service, providing no fewer than fifteen trains between Portsmouth Harbour – sensibly taking precedence over Southsea now, be it noted – and Cardiff Central, all via Southampton Central and Bristol Temple Meads. The provision is hourly from 0723 following an early departure at 0600. Journey time generally is 2hr 20min, though the last train of the day, the 2023 from Portsmouth, takes a little over 2½ hours. Closure of the less-well-patronised stations, mostly west of Salisbury, has obviously affected the stopping pattern. However, the major calling points are much as before, and Bradford-on-Avon's status has obviously risen in the operator's estimation because it now features in all workings.

FGW also offers three services between Southampton and Bristol TM in 2 hours, and two others from Brighton, one at each end of the day, to the same destination. The timing of those is around 3½ hours. South West Trains adds four more between Salisbury and Bristol TM in a minute under 2 hours. The total passing through Westbury on such workings is thus about twice the number sixty years ago. Moreover, it illustrates how travel demand has altered, with a regular-interval service throughout the day. That change is much clearer when considering the Sunday service, for as many trains run through on that day as did so on a 1953 summer Saturday. On Sundays now Brighton gets three 'through' services to Bristol, one of which continues to Cardiff, though it's a 4½-hour journey.

It is as well to recall also that the Summer Saturday trains in 1953 were possibly up to ten coaches long at times, a contrast to the two or three of today's Class 158 units. Even in the 1970s photographic evidence shows that six or seven 'standard' coaches behind a modest 'diesel' – Classes 31, 33 and 35 are all pictured – was the norm. Plus ça change!

Ringwood

Ringwood, situated about halfway along 'Castleman's Corkscrew' between Brockenhurst and Wimborne, was very much on the main line until Bournemouth came on the scene. With the opening of the direct line from Brockenhurst to Branksome, it started a new life as a rural backwater, but also as a useful diversionary route until rationalisation of the rail network in the 1960s saw an end to first passenger, then freight traffic. It is interesting how the word 'rationalisation' can be used to both justify the terms 'with logical reason' and 'to make more efficient', thus dispensing with what at the time was considered the superfluous. Fifty years later we may still question how so many parts of the rail network were got rid of with relatively short-sighted justification. Unfortunately these actions seemed logical to the powers that held sway at the time, powers with no positive vision of how the future of such nationalised assets might be used.

The images offered here were taken (unless otherwise stated) by the late Norman Pattenden. I suspect they formed part of his research for a possible modelling project, and depict the scene at Ringwood in September 1966, just a few months before closure on 8 January 1967.

Ringwood's goods shed, looking rather the worse for wear, is an example of the type of LSWR shed built for access at 90 degrees to the main line via a wagon turntable through what here would have been an arch at the left-hand end of the building. Later in its life, a hole has been punched through the side wall, cutting into the window arches, with an 'I'-section beam supporting the roof over the opening. The corrugated grain store (provender store) to the right stands on characteristic concrete staddle stones. Note how the white line at the platform edge of the up platform peters out at the top of the ramp.

The east end of the station is seen here with 'disarmed' signals, a string of mineral wagons and a few vans, including one Southern Railway vehicle. The Exmouth Junction concrete slabs edging the down platform have been removed since the end of passenger services. Did they get recycled into some suburban platform lengthening projects that were popular around this time?

This picture acts as a link between the first two and the store on the extreme left and the mineral wagons overlapping to the right. Like the goods shed, Ground Frame B seems to have suffered the attention of the local stone-throwers. Some bits of Exmouth Junction product are parked under the steps and will probably never be involved in 'active service'.

Ground Frame B is seen here in more detail, showing the targeted windows, missing slates and broken valance. The porch too seems to be hanging off the main structure. This would be a difficult feature to model as it would just not look right, as if the modeller could not make it square.

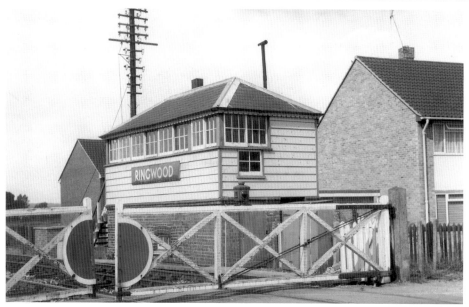

The more publicly located signal box next to the level crossing seems to have fared rather better than Ground Frame B. It is labelled on the back of the original photograph as 'Ringwood A', a statement that reflects the now reduced status of the signal box to a ground frame on 5 September 1965. This SRS classified Type 1 box has an extra window to allow the signalman to see the state of the crossing while turning the gate wheel. Indeed, this end of the box was extended in 1904 when additional levers and the gate wheel were added, the vertical join for which may be discerned in the different materials from the top of the windows down to the ground.. Thus the near end of the building lacks a locking room window; the two (one behind the gate target) are to the left of the two window slides with smaller panes, which indicate the location of the original end of the box.

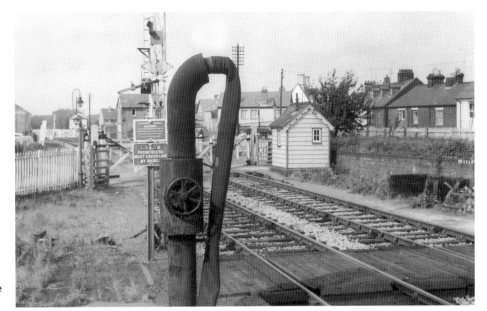

The water column, mixed SR and LSWR warning notices and the boarded barrow crossing are seen from the west end of the down platform. Beyond this is a gate hut and the first set of gates, while the signal box and the level crossing can be seen further to the west. Road traffic queues at these crossings did little encourage positive relations between the railway and the community.

The extensive canopy over the up platform blocks most of the view of the station building. The bowstring girder, open-sided footbridge can be seen at the western end.

The down platform, porters' board crossing and a lot of SR concrete is to be seen here. In the darkness to the right is the loop line running behind the platform, as seen in the next image.

The wooden pent-roofed building, complete with its complement of fire buckets, extends beyond the end of the brick station building with its roof ventilators. This itself extends beyond the flat part of the canopy that gives way to the more elaborate roof over the loop line.

The back end of a short down freight train stands waiting for the gates to be opened for the railway.

With both sets of gates open, the Class 33 (Type 3) is moving forward, taking the train towards West Moors. This part of the route was still open then, even though the track to the east had been closed to traffic. Ringwood was therefore the temporary terminus of the line, which was now worked as a long siding.

While Norman Pattenden's pictures depict the scene at Ringwood in September 1966, this image is clearly earlier, and may have been taken by someone other than Norman. The presence of passengers and the 'at the ready' platform trolley suggests that the station was still open. The 'Q' Class 0-6-0 is arriving from the west with a goods that includes a potentially large fitted head.

Whilst preparing this piece from Maurice we also came across three colour views of the infrastructure, which add to the flavour of the location. No dates are given but, as can be seen, it is prior to when the signalling was removed and therefore likely to be when the railway was fully open.

The first, taken from the station footbridge, is looking west towards Ashley Heath and what had also been the junction for the line to Hurn and Christchurch before its closure in 1935. Prior to this time there had been three running lines over both level crossings, the third line on the left coming from the loop platform at the station and running where the grass can see to the point of divergence. Ringwood West signal box may be seen in the distance with a ground frame hut for the crossing nearest the camera. The tall co-acting stop signal had once included a bracket part way up the post for the Christchurch line.

Ground Frame B was at the east end of the station and was designated as such from 20 January 1929. Originally provided with a 13-lever frame, a number of levers would have been redundant after 1929.

A short distance east of Ringwood Ground Frame 'B', at the end of the up and down sidings, was yet another level crossing at Crow Lane, controlled from the ground frame hut seen here. 'Ringwood No 16 Crossing' was numbered as one of the numerous crossing huts and associated cottages on the original 'Castleman's Corkscrew' route. Not a block post, the hut contained five levers, including control/slotting for the up and down home signals.

Southern Camping Coaches
Part 1 1935-48

Mike King

The idea of railway camping coaches originated with the LNER, which in 1933 converted ten elderly six-wheeled vehicles and placed them at various holiday sites in Yorkshire, Cumberland and Westmorland. For around £2 10s 0d per week, holidaymakers could enjoy their basic but clean facilities at scenic locations convenient for rail travel – not only at the start and end of their holiday, but also during their week's stay. Predictably the other 'Big Four' companies soon followed the LNER's lead, the first Southern coach being exhibited at various London termini in February and March 1935. Such was the popularity of the scheme that by 1939 there were well in excess of 400 such coaches up and down the country, although by this time the SR stock numbered just twenty-four vehicles, a total that would remain constant until 1960.

Part of the deal was that customers had to make their way to the sites using rail travel. In the days before mass car ownership this would have been the norm anyway, and the hire of a typical four-berth coach would also require the purchase of not fewer than three adult (two child fares counted as one adult) return tickets as well – and this would almost certainly have been the most expensive part of the holiday. Pro-rata arrangements applied for six- or eight-berth coaches. For this reason (with a one-off notable exception) the

This is the original 'Exhibition Camping Coach' No 1, as exhibited at London termini during February and March 1935. Formerly LCDR 28-foot Third No 45, built at Longhedge in June 1892, it was renumbered as SECR 2999 in February 1903 and as SR 1661 in December 1926, then ran in fourteen-coach excursion set 834 until withdrawal on 1 December 1934, based latterly at Sevenoaks. It became camping coach No 1 in January 1935. The bedrooms are on the left, with beds across the vehicle, the living room is in the centre, and the kitchen at the right, with the 50-gallon water tank directly beneath. Its final location was Combpyne, on the Lyme Regis branch, in 1950-53. *SR Official*

Southern chose to locate most coaches remote from the capital, i.e. in Devon and Cornwall, in order to maximise revenue. As one SR officer was heard to remark, 'We do not want customers travelling to Wimbledon Common with a 9d return – we want at least four good long-distance return fares as well!' The notable exception was during Coronation Week in May 1937, when attractions in and around London caused something of a temporary rethink. Visitors wishing to see the Coronation of King George VI and Queen Elizabeth were offered several coaches parked at Tattenham Corner station. The other companies moved coaches to other suitable suburban stations in a similar manner. All charged premium prices, well in excess of double the normal hire rates.

The greatest downside, to modern eyes at least, was that lavatory facilities were not provided in the coaches themselves – punters were expected to use the station toilets! This would most certainly not be a selling point today, but back then things were different and the lack of en-suite facilities was not seen as a deterrent. Of course, in those days the stations were immaculately maintained and no doubt the lavatories at country stations were probably little-used first thing in the morning. Heating, lighting and cooking facilities were basic – but the Southern did at least provide pumped water and later electricity, services not always matched by the other companies who stuck to paraffin oil, later Calor gas, and water drawn from the station supply. The Southern also advertised the provision of a wireless aerial, although customers had to provide their own radio – the 1930s equivalent of Wi-Fi! Also provided was an alarm clock, but one hopes that its use was optional.

The first twelve SR conversions were ex-LCDR six-wheelers, authorised in December 1934 (HOO E837) and completed rapidly between January and April 1935. Interestingly, their numbers are shown as S1-12, but in fact the numbers applied were not prefixed in any way until BR days. Apart from No 2, all were former 28-foot five-compartment Thirds to SR Diagram 88. No 2 was the exception, being a 30-foot ex-Second to Diagram 86. Just why this one was different is not known, but it was presumably conveniently available. At that time many ex-LCDR six-wheelers were being withdrawn from excursion traffic so there would have been a plentiful supply from which to select. Perhaps the difference was not realised until work on the 30-foot vehicle had been started.

Coach No 1 was exhibited at Waterloo station during the week commencing 18 February 1935, moving then to Victoria and later London Bridge in order to publicise the new venture. The March 1935 issue of *The Southern Railway Magazine* included a short article and a picture of 'campers' taking tea on the platform alongside the coach at Waterloo. The Topical Press Agency was also invited, and its pictures showed morning tea being served in bed – but in 1935 the lady in the bed was, of course, fully clothed! The exhibition was judged a success, as many members of the public took time to view the coach and quite a number of bookings were taken. The sites initially selected for the summer of 1935 were in Cornwall, Devon and Hampshire and were publicised as follows:

Umberleigh – for North Devon

Otterham – for North Cornwall

Gunnislake – for the Tamar Valley

Brentor – for Dartmoor

Bridestowe – for Dartmoor

Newton Poppleford – for East Devon

Woodbury Road – for East Devon

Hurn – for the New Forest

With twelve coaches available, some locations had two coaches. Most locations were re-used in subsequent years; however, the Christchurch-Ringwood line closed on 30 September 1935 so Hurn was not selected again. Other locations were later added – especially once the stock of coaches was doubled – but uniquely in 1938 some coaches were moved mid-season, giving a total of twenty-four pre-war sites. This was done only in 1938 so was presumably not a runaway success. The LNER had tried this flexible approach in 1933 and 1934 only, but by 1935 each location became fixed for the entire summer season. The LNER also tried just one 'touring camping coach', which moved around a number of Yorkshire Dales sites during the week, attached to scheduled passenger services, allowing holidaymakers to sample several locations as part of a week-long tour, but this enterprise was never adopted by the other companies. The use of Tattenham Corner during May 1937 has already been mentioned, but after 1938 the Southern also stuck to permanent locations for the duration of each summer.

Opposite: **'Old carriage bodies for sale'** – from the *South Western Railway Magazine* of 1922.

Camping coaches Nos 1-12

Camping Coach No	Former identity	Built by	Converted	Withdrawn
1	D88 28ft Third 1661	LCDR 6/92	1/35	3/54
2	D86 30ft Second 1619	LCDR 2/87	4/35	3/54
3	D88 28ft Third 1675	LCDR 1/96	4/35	3/54
4	D88 28ft Third 1682	LCDR 1/96	4/35	3/54
5	D88 28ft Third 1687	LCDR 12/95	4/35	3/54
6	D88 28ft Third 1704	LCDR 11/96	4/35	3/54
7	D88 28ft Third 1728	LCDR 12/92	4/35	3/54
8	D88 28ft Third 1736	LCDR 2/91	3/35	6/46
9	D88 28ft Third 1742	LCDR 3/91	4/35	3/54
10	D88 28ft Third 1753	LCDR 10/91	4/35	3/54
11	D88 28ft Third 1764	LCDR 3/97	4/35	3/54
12	D88 28ft Third 1767	LCDR 3/97	4/35	3/46

S.W. Carriage used as Living Quarters. Fitted with bed, couch, piano, etc.

OLD CARRIAGE BODIES FOR SALE.

In the sidings at Micheldever there are frequently to be seen a number of weatherworn coaches of obsolete design which have obviously reached that stage when they could no longer be used for traffic purposes. Their railway day is done, yet as is the case with many of the old Guards who have travelled thousands of miles with them, years of useful life still remain for them after their last working trip is finished.

Old carriage bodies are in constant demand by those who know that by a little ingenuity they can be readily adapted for many purposes. In playing fields they form excellent dressing-rooms for football and cricket clubs, along the river banks a close inspection of some of the picturesque bungalows will reveal that an old railway carriage has been transformed; for outhouses, stores and suchlike useful if less ornamental purposes, old carriage bodies are eminently suitable; even dwelling-house accommodation has been contrived for them, and at Byfleet an enterprising butcher uses an old L. & S.W. goods wagon as his shop.

How can the public obtain possession of an old carriage body, and what is the cost? There is no difficulty whatever in any club or private individual obtaining possession of an old South-Western carriage. From the sidings at Micheldever, batches of old stock are worked to the Carriage Shops at Eastleigh. There they are stripped of all gas-fittings and trimmings, made weather-proof, given a coat of paint, and are ready for sale. At the present time the Carriage and Wagon Department, Eastleigh, have for disposal, at £20 each, a number of old carriage bodies, 30 ft. long by 8 ft. wide, with five compartments. They can be inspected at Eastleigh by arrangement with Mr. S. Warner, the Carriage Superintendent.

The price of £20 includes conveyance on their own underframe to any South-Western station. The purchaser is required to remove the body from the underframe, which latter is returned to Eastleigh for further service.

This removal is rendered easy, as the bolts, etc., are loosened by the Carriage Department before the vehicle leaves Eastleigh. A couple of men with a trolley can easily transport the body to the field or site desired, and there the old coach, which has spent 20 or 30 years of wearing, tearing and roaming, finally settles down to a more peaceful experience.

COACH BODY FOR SALE £20

One of several ready for sale.

The unique 30-foot former Second Class vehicle 1619, now camping coach No 2 and possibly in SR malachite green, stands at Umberleigh in June 1948. This was the oldest coach to be converted, dating from 1887, and features the earlier style of half-round beading on waist and upper panels. Note the original SR number painted on the end – this was standard practice. This coach was later noted at Newton Poppleford and finally at Amberley in 1953. *J. H. Aston*

Details of the original twelve ex-LCDR coaches are given in the accompanying table. Each was divided into three separate compartments, comprising a living room, a compact kitchen area and sleeping accommodation for six persons – with washbasins in the sleeping compartments. Water was pumped to these and to the kitchen tap from a 50-gallon tank mounted under one end of the vehicle. In this respect at least, the Southern vehicles were better served than equivalent coaches on the GWR, LMS and LNER. Hire costs were £2 10s 0d per week between 1 April and 30 June, and £3 10s 0d per week between 1 July and 30 September. The usual arrangements for travel applied, with no fewer than the equivalent of four adult return tickets from the home station needing to be purchased.

Camping coaches Nos 13-24

Camping Coach No	Former identity	Built by	Converted	Withdrawn
13	D273 50ft Compo 5019	LSWR 12/01	5/36	12/60
14	D273 50ft Compo 5023	LSWR 6/01	5/36	12/60
15	D273 50ft Compo 5026	LSWR 6/01	5/36	12/60*
16	D273 50ft Compo 5027	LSWR 6/01	5/36	12/60
17	D273 50ft Compo 5030	LSWR 12/01	4/36	4/48
18	D273 50ft Compo 5032	LSWR 12/01	6/36	12/60
19	D16 50ft Second 598	LSWR 6/02	12/38	1/61
20	D16 50ft Second 599	LSWR 6/02	12/38	1/62
21	D117 50ft Brake Third 2753	LSWR 3/02	3/39	1/62
22	D272 50ft Compo 4989	LSWR 10/00	3/39	1/62
23	D273 50ft Compo 5017	LSWR 12/01	3/39	1/62
24	D273 50ft Compo 5022	LSWR 12/01	3/39	1/62

* Coach 15 was subsequently used for departmental purposes, firstly at Barnstaple Junction and finally at Southampton Terminus in 1965.

The most numerous bogie camping coach type was the LSWR Diagram 273 50-foot Composite, with eight examples converted between April 1936 and March 1939. No 17 was formerly Composite 5030 and was the first of these conversions. It is seen in Littleham goods yard, probably in 1937 or perhaps during the following two years, as it displays the pre-war lettering style. Note the sleepers placed across the track at both ends, just to make sure nobody shunted it anywhere! This was one of the coaches that failed to return to service after the war; withdrawal is recorded as April 1948, but whether it suffered wartime damage while in staff use at Orpington is not certain. One official record seen by the author states that three coaches – Nos 8, 12 and 17 – were damaged by enemy action, but withdrawal dates quoted vary between March 1946 and April 1948, so the 'enemy action' record may not be correct.

As ever, the Southern was cautious about the new venture, but experience through the 1935 season showed that larger vehicles would be beneficial. Accordingly the next batch of six, authorised in February 1936 (order E905), was converted from ex-LSWR 50-foot Lavatory Composites – not that the lavatories were retained! These still accommodated six persons but were available for an increased hire rate of up to £4 per week, depending on the time of year; and these prices, including the differentiation between six-wheeled and bogie vehicles, remained unchanged until wartime restrictions caused the scheme to be curtailed. The six-wheelers were referred to as Type A, and the bogie vehicles were Type B. Six more ex-LSWR bogie coaches were authorised in October 1938 (order E1051), and these were ready for the 1939 summer season. This time only two were identical to the 1936 Diagram 273 conversions – the others were former Thirds, a Brake Third and a different type of Composite to Diagrams 16, 117 and 272. Details are given in the accompanying table.

Pre-war sites

As already noted, Hurn station was not used after the 1935 season, but the other seven sites continued together with sixteen others, as shown in the table, which soon reveals which sites proved to be the most popular. Some late arrivals to the list were destined to remain in favour right through to the end of the service, while others were tried once only, never to reappear.

Coaches Nos 6 (ex-1704) and 11 (ex-1764) at East Budleigh on 29 June 1948. These are not actually on rails but are standing on old sleepers, yet they were clearly moved at the end of the season as both were subsequently noted at other locations. *J. H. Aston*

Camping coach locations, 1935

FS refers to full season – April-September in 1935, April-October thereafter – otherwise as noted.

Location	1935	1936	1937	1938	1939
Amberley (Sussex)	–	–	–	April, May, October	FS
Ardingly (Sussex)	–	–	–	April, May, October	–
Bere Ferrers (Devon)	–	FS	FS	June, July, August	FS
Brentor (Devon)	FS	FS	–	–	FS
Bridestowe (Devon)	FS	FS	FS	June, July, August	FS
East Budleigh (Devon)	–	–	FS	FS	FS
East Farleigh (Kent)	–	–	–	April, May, October	–
Gunnislake (Cornwall)	FS	FS	FS	June, July, August	FS
Hinton Admiral (Hants)	–	–	–	April, May, October	FS
Hurn (Hants)	FS	–	–	–	–
Littleham (Devon)	–	–	FS	June, July, August	FS
Lyndhurst Road (Hants)	–	FS	FS	FS	FS
Martin Mill (Kent)	–	–	–	April, May, October	FS
Newick & Chailey (Sussex)	–	–	–	April, May, October	–
Newington (Kent)	–	–	–	April, May, October	–
Newton Poppleford (Devon)	FS	FS	FS	June, July, August	FS
Otterham (Cornwall)	FS	FS	FS	June, July, August	FS
Port Isaac Road (Cornwall)	–	–	FS	June, July, August	FS
Sandling Junction (Kent)	–	–	–	–	FS
Selling (Kent)	–	–	–	April, May, October	–
South Molton Road (Devon)	–	FS	–	–	–
Umberleigh (Devon)	FS	FS	FS	June, July, August	FS
Woodbury Road (Devon)	FS	FS	FS	FS	FS
Wool (Dorset)	–	FS	FS	FS	FS

One of the later bogie conversions was Diagram 273 LSWR Composite 5032, outshopped as camping coach No 18 in June 1936. The bedrooms are nearest, with the beds set out lengthways, the kitchen at the far end, and the much larger living room in the centre. Note the exemplary paint finish – complete with varnished teak droplights, exactly mirroring the finish applied at that time to main-line stock. This coach was later noted at Port Isaac Road and Wrafton. *SR Official*

LSWR bogie camping coach No 16, LCDR coach No 2 and one other arrive at Salisbury station on their way from Eastleigh Works to the West in May 1936. The photographer captioned the reverse 'en route to Cornwall'. The bogie vehicle is newly converted, while the LCDR coaches are about to start their second season of operation and look to have at least been revarnished before dispatch. They are clearly at the rear of a stopping train bound for Exeter. *J. G. Griffiths*

Some coaches returned to the same site year on year but, due to the policy of returning the vehicles to workshops for maintenance and overhauls during the winter, some 'did the rounds' of available sites over a period of years. However, Amberley, Newton Poppleford and East Budleigh at least seemed to favour the Type A ex-LCDR six-wheelers until they were phased out at the end of the 1953 season – usually two per site. Unfortunately, information on which coaches served where before the war is lacking, so a definitive list cannot be provided. The late Roger Kidner photographed Nos 10 and 12 at Newton Poppleford in 1936 and noted no fewer than four at the 'one-off' site of East Farleigh in the spring of 1938; however, whether all were in use is not known.

Wartime changes

Despite what might have been expected, all four companies again advertised the coaches for hire for the summer of 1940, although just how many lets were actually taken up is unknown. Early that year, during the period of the 'Phoney War', clearly some people were still in a position to consider booking a holiday; however, once the Blitz began this may have waned rapidly as other considerations took precedence. Once the railways came under Government control, the Railway Executive Committee (REC) soon looked at alternative uses for camping coaches. The National Archives at Kew hold much correspondence between the REC and the railway companies on the subject – and it is evident that neither universal agreement nor cooperation was achieved, at least not for a

while. As early as mid-September 1939 the REC considered to what uses the vehicles might lend themselves – countrywide they amounted to some 439 vehicles, so the matter was not insubstantial. The Committee's recommendation was that the coaches be stored at various locations ready for use in an emergency. Primarily this was expected to be for displaced railway staff, military authorities or Government departments. The railways countered this by stating that many bookings were already in place for the next year, and that these should be allowed to stand, at least for the present time.

By June 1940, of the 439 vehicles some seventy were already in railway departmental use, 120 for Government requests (including for naval and military purposes), fifty were vacant and available for use, and, perhaps surprisingly, 199 were still booked by holidaymakers. The position as far as the Southern was concerned on 10 July 1940 was:

Booked by holidaymakers	4
In use by Government/navy/military	8
In use by the railway	12
Total	24

The four that were booked could be released as soon as the present lets were over. Their locations are not known but almost certainly in the West of England.

However, there were rumblings of disquiet from the railway companies as to what uses the vehicles were being put. Accusations were made that the coaches were simply being used as dormitories for military personnel rather than any semblance of emergency use, and that ordinary condemned coaches would be better used as mere dormitories. The railways' view was that the coaches would be better deployed to protect vulnerable installations such as tunnels, bridges and viaducts in locations where other accommodation was not available, manned either by Home Guard or railway personnel, or a combination of both. With the threat of invasion now imminent, these were important considerations. Once the Blitz started, the Ministry of Health investigated the possibility of using the coaches for bombed-out families, but in fact this use was restricted just to key railway staff who found themselves in this position. The situation was ever-changing and by November 1940 almost all the SR vehicles were in some form of departmental use, a situation that was to remain largely unchanged for the duration of the war, despite what may have been happening elsewhere. Two SR coaches were loaned to the Hampshire County War Agricultural Committee and one more was in use by the RAF to man a balloon barrage, both these arrangements being in force during 1941. The other three companies continued to receive various requests for the coaches – some were agreed, others rebuffed. Gradually all vehicles were reclaimed by the railway companies, but some were beyond further service and were soon condemned – this occurred to just three of the Southern examples.

Wartime camping coach locations

Location	Coach Nos
Eastleigh	1, 8, 9, 11, 21, 24
Ringwood	3, 11 (later at Eastleigh), 20
Romsey	23
Redhill	13, 15
Victoria Sidings	5
Woking	4
Paddock Wood	10
Micheldever	16
Rotherhithe Road	8 (later at Eastleigh)
Chichester	12
Orpington	17

Some noted locations for the vehicles during the latter part and just after the war are shown in the table. Some remained in worn and faded Maunsell green with the 'Camping Coach' legend visible, while others were light grey. Nos 8, 12 and 17 all failed to return to camping coach service.

Post-war revival

Only the Southern managed to reinstate the camping coach service prior to nationalisation – on the other regions of British Railways this would wait until 1952. Several sites in Sussex, Dorset, Devon and Cornwall were advertised for the summer of 1947; with the coach numbers noted for that year at each site in brackets, the sites included Amberley (No 2), Corfe Castle (a Type A six-wheeler), Gunnislake (No 23), Port Isaac Road (No 18), Wrafton (Nos 20 and 22), Woodbury Road (No 16), and Wool (No 13), and there may have been others. Notice that just two of the former LCDR vehicles have so far appeared, and all sites except Corfe Castle and Wrafton had been used previously. Bere Ferrers, Lyndhurst Road, East Budleigh, Newton Poppleford, Otterham, Umberleigh, Sandling Junction, Littleham, Hinton Admiral and three new sites, Whitstone & Bridgerule, Combpyne and Tipton St Johns, would be added in 1948. For Gunnislake, Otterham and Umberleigh this may have been their final year, while individual coaches appear to have moved around somewhat between 1947 and 1949, probably as overhauls were completed at Eastleigh Works. Part 2 of this article will start with details of the 1948 sites and the coaches noted at each. Post-war prices varied between £5 and £9 per week, depending on the type of coach and the time of year, there now being low, medium and high season rates.

To replace the three vehicles lost and return the stock to twenty-four vehicles, three more conversions were authorised in January 1947, under order E3398. However, there appears to be some confusion over the actual dates of conversion and two more vehicles were earmarked as well – one of which would become a camping coach but under a slightly different arrangement. The details are given in the accompanying table.

All these were rather different from what had gone before. No 25 was a former LSWR clerestory-roofed restaurant car that had been rebuilt as an elliptical-roofed unclassed saloon in May 1931. It was further converted into Naval Ambulance Coach WD1240 for the Admiralty in July 1943, but was returned to the Southern in 1946 in time for conversion into a rather splendid-looking camping coach, taking up station at Hinton Admiral for the 1948 season. Nos 26 and 27 were the first ex-SECR Wainwright coaches to be converted, and both

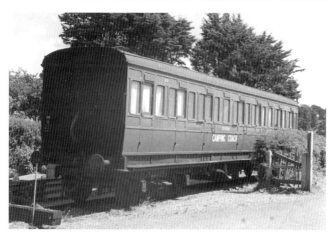

Diagram 16 50-foot Second (later Third) 599, now camping coach No 20, stands in picturesque surroundings at Woodbury Road on 29 June 1948 (the station was renamed Exton in September 1958). The River Exe estuary is behind the photographer. Considering that there were just eight examples of this diagram, it is perhaps remarkable that two survived as camping coaches. No 20 was at Wrafton in the previous year, but was a regular at Woodbury Road in the 1950s. *J. H. Aston*

Camping coaches Nos 25-29

Camping Coach No	Former identity	Built by	Converted	Withdrawn
25	D593 56ft Saloon 7828	LSWR 5/07	3/48	1/62
26	D493 51ft 1in Saloon 7365	Metro/SECR 9/09	2/47 or 3/48?	1/62
27	D47 46ft Second 933	Metro/SECR 4/00	7/46 or 3/48?	1/62
28	D597 56ft Dining Car 7840	LSWR 5/10	Not converted	–
29	D622 50ft 2in Saloon 7930	Metro/SECR 3/03	9/47	2/63

Right: Well and truly in the wilds! This is former Brake Third 2753 as camping coach No 21 at the far end of Port Isaac Road sidings on 3 July 1948. Jim Aston certainly got about during that week!! By the early 1950s this coach had become the usual resident at Corfe Castle. *J. H. Aston*

Below: At Corfe Castle on 12 June 1948 is Diagram 272 50-foot Tri-composite 4989, now renumbered as camping coach No 22. It is probably in malachite and was at Wrafton in the previous year; it would return there subsequently, ending its days at Littleham in 1961. *J. H. Aston*

A rather later picture at Littleham shows SECR coach S26S (BR numbering style) on 20 September 1961, now in Southern Region green livery. By this time there were no fewer than four coaches at this station, the others being Nos 22, 23 and 27. One of the LSWR pair may just be seen behind. On the coach end is the number 958 – confusingly, this should read departmental No 1958s, but some digits have been painted out. The large side windows show that this was once a saloon coach – First Class No 7365 – before its departmental days. *A. E. West*

had previously served since 1943/44 as departmental coaches 1958s and 1932s respectively. Their withdrawal from these duties and conversion appears to have been the February 1947 and July 1946 dates given in the table. They were sent to Tipton St Johns and Sandling Junction respectively, also for the 1948 season. Coach 7840 was another LSWR former clerestory-roofed restaurant car that had also been rebuilt with an elliptical roof in 1935 but had remained as a dining vehicle.

This probably spent some of the war as a mobile canteen and was withdrawn from these duties in May 1946, so would probably have been on hand at Eastleigh when the next conversions were being considered. One register seen by the writer shows that this vehicle was intended to become camping coach No 28, but in the event this failed to take place and presumably the coach was scrapped instead. This camping coach number was destined to remain blank.

At the other end of the system is coach No 27 – ex-SECR seven-compartment Second (later Third) 933 – at Sandling Junction in 1948. This does carry its former departmental number (1932s) on the end. In 1960 a Pullman camping coach was installed here and No 27 moved to Littleham. *Author's collection*

Certainly the most impressive camping coach available for public use was No 25, converted in March 1948 from ex-LSWR restaurant car 7828 and seen here at Hinton Admiral on 13 June 1948 during its first season of operation. It carries malachite green livery, still with the company title visible, despite having been converted three months after the Southern Railway ceased to exist. It later served at Wool and Bere Ferrers together with one of the 1953 conversions, to be described in Part 2. *J. H. Aston*

Camping coach No 29 was also destined to remain blank – at least officially. Unofficially the number was allocated to former SECR Royal Saloon 7930, purchased by SR Operating Department officer Sidney W. Smart in September 1947. 'Smartie', as he was known, was an avid fisherman and the coach usually resided in a remote part of Newhaven Harbour sidings, although when freshly converted it was seen at Littlehampton Harbour sidings in February 1948, almost certainly for the same purpose. It remained in his private use for some 15 years, at first retaining its olive green livery, but by about 1955 it was repainted in very pale grey with a gleaming white roof. Periodically the coach would be returned to Lancing for refurbishment and its appearance at such places as Lewes or Brighton would confound enthusiasts unaware

of its continued existence. It was last noted in for repainting during 1960 and never visibly carried the number 29 – just the former running number 7930 stencilled on the solebar. After return to BR in 1963 it was reconditioned as Scottish Region 'Pullman Camping Coach' SC51 and allocated to Glenfinnan, where it outlived all other SR camping coaches, serving until 1969.

Part 2 will take the story up to the 1960s, including the Pullman camping coach era, but before continuing I would like to thank photographer Jim Aston for making such a comprehensive record of West Country camping coaches during his summer 1948 holiday. No fewer than six illustrate this part of the article, just over a third of those actually photographed.

'Smartie's coach', the former SECR Royal Saloon 7930, poses at Newhaven Harbour sidings in 1955, shortly after being repainted at Lancing in light grey livery. It also appears to be connected to mains drainage and has the benefit of an electricity supply. It isn't what you know, it's who you know! It is believed much of the former Royal interior remained in the coach at this time and, clearly, it is being well cared for. *D. B. Clayton*

Rebuilt
The letters and comments pages

As with all things computer-orientated, sometimes there will be a crash. For this reason, and mindful of an event some years ago when we did lose a lot of files (including all those of *SW3*), we have been backing up everything for some time. However, on attempting to access the back-up that too has failed with the result that the air was a bit 'blue' for a time. Fortunately a friendly computer expert was able to assist, but while he was able to recover an awful lot, the original file names have corrupted, so we cannot be certain which has been used and which not! On the basis, then, of apologies if it has been seen before, we present the old-fashioned guard at work. We have no idea as to the type of carriage, although something makes me think it could be a COR or similar. Any offers?

As ever, a 'bumper-bundle' of comments, corrections and general extra information has arisen from past issues. We start with a long-term friend of 'SW', Frank Spence:

'Accident at Hastings Station – 4 June 1957. During the mid to late 1950s we would spend our holidays with my Aunt in Hastings. As she worked in the morning my mother would prepare lunch while Dad and I would head into the town to do any shopping that was required. However, if shopping was not required we would wander down to the Old Town to see Jim Hughes, who managed the Hastings Miniature Railway for Ian Allan, a much preferable option!

Aunt lived in Wykeham Road and her property backed onto Linton Gardens, to which she had direct access through a gate at the bottom of her garden. On the day in question Dad decided we would go through the Gardens to Braybrooke Terrace, a road that ran parallel to the railway between Linton Road Bridge and Hastings Station, and then into town.

As we were walking towards Braybrooke Terrace an EMU went by towards the station and moments later there was a loud bang and crunching sound. As we left the entrance to the Gardens we could clearly see that a 'Schools' Class locomotive had collided tender-first with the EMU and a large brown dust cloud hung over the scene. Had we been a couple of seconds earlier we would have witnessed the actual crash and, as an eight-year-old, the sight that greeted us was one I have never forgotten. I am sure a report of the incident was published in the *Hastings and St Leonards Observer* at the time.

I never did take the number of the 'School' that caused the accident but, thanks to the article on *SW31*, I now know the date and, more importantly, I can cross off 30932 in my much-worn Ian Allan *abc*. (It crossed my mind that *Blundells* would require works attention and I consulted Richard Derry's *Book of the Schools* (Irwell Press). This might help: 'Following the accident *Blundells* was sent to Ashford Works and admitted for repair on 13 June 1957. This was described as a Non-Classified Light Casual and the locomotive was released on 21 June, implying the damage was relatively minor.')

Moving on to the photographs of Petworth (*SW31*, p48), they also remind me that Billy Smart's Circus visited Hastings and the stock was berthed in the goods yard, easily visible from the South Terrace Bridge at the east end of the station. Maybe the Petworth photographs were taken the same year as the train's visit to Hastings, probably in August?

Hastings goods yard was also the venue for one of the new DEMUs to be displayed in 1957 coinciding with a stay with my Aunt. Steps were provided at the front and rear driver's doors so you could enter at one end and progress through the engine room, along the train and out at the other end. Needless to say as it was brand new and both engine rooms were immaculate so there was no risk of getting any oil on one's clothes.'

From Tony Logan concerning the (4COR) Portsmouth and mid-Sussex stock.

'During the war, once catering services were withdrawn, the buffet cars were withdrawn from the 4BUF units and stored. Several were stabled in the up-side sidings (but downhill!) at Crystal Palace High Level; unfortunately it was not possible to recognise their numbers from passing trains. (Pre-war these sidings were home to three 'birdcage' long sets for excursion and holiday relief traffic; they returned after the war.) All the buffet cars were in pre-war version malachite (as No 925 *Cheltenham* currently). The assertion that any were painted in Maunsell green is suspect, I think. After the war they were repainted in post-war malachite (as No 777 *Sir Lamiel*), and restored to units similarly treated.

'The restaurant cars remained in the 4RES units during the war. I remember a journey to Portsmouth Harbour in 1945, when I travelled in the Third Class restaurant. The bomb-damaged unit 3132 was a sorry sight, marooned in part of the Harbour station.

Hayling Farewell. Reference to Bradley's *LB&SCR Locos*, Vol 1, would have been a good idea before publishing the list of locos on page 95. No locos were ever numbered 32654/72 or 82. In 1898 the Newhaven Harbour Company purchased No 72 *Fenchurch*, before it had been added to the duplicate list as 672. It returned to the Southern in 1927. It was given a vacant number, 2636, rather than the more logical 2672. It remained allocated to Newhaven and was the oldest extant 'Terrier'. It's now based at Sheffield Park. No 2654 (or was it still B654?) was transferred to service stock in 1932 as No 680S and allocated to Lancing Works. Withdrawn in 1962, it is now in Canada, having been restored at Eastleigh as No 54 *Waddon*. Likewise, No 2682 (B682) became Brighton Works shunter as No 380S. Withdrawn in 1946, it was restored at Brighton as No 82 *Boxhill* and is part of our National collection.

D. L. Bradley's books provide a wealth of information about the locomotives of the Southern and its constituent companies, including a lot more about the Terriers.'

We think this is the former *Boxhill* (see the letter from Tony Logan) after restoration and recorded at the front of Eastleigh Works. The BR numberplate appears to survive while the engine name has yet to be added.

Now from Graham Buxton-Smither:

'Hello. I rarely feel compelled to write to organisations these days unless to complain, but I really wanted to thank all those concerned with *The Southern Way* for the quality of the publication and the pleasure it has given me.

My dedication to the Southern – sadly too young for Southern Railway, so it had to be the Southern Region – was secured at a tiny station in Surrey called Salfords (between Earlswood and Horley), which as you know started life as a Halt. I used to pass near it on my way to prep school every day and got to know the delightful Mr Sweet, who was Station Master (at least that was how he appeared to be to me) back in the mid-fifties. There was a small goods yard there, largely servicing the Hall & Co coal depot, and on a glorious summer's day I played hookey from school (it never occurred to me that I'd be missed!) after the driver and fireman offered me a ride on their footplate; I was in heaven. I recall it was a tender locomotive and was collecting a number of wooden and metal coal wagons; I was so excited by the occasion. I still recall having to be hauled up onto the footplate as I couldn't even reach the first step; then being made eggs and bacon on the shovel and a mug of tea – nothing ever tasted so good. After about an hour they said they had to get on with their work and let me down to the ground – I was covered in oil, coal dust, smuts and bacon grease and from that moment all I wanted to be was a steam engine driver... I won't dwell on the trouble I got into when I arrived home, the school having rung to enquire as to my health...

Some years later I got to travel on a footplate again, that time on the short journey from Redhill to Reigate following a diesel failure; I was so surprised to hear the hiss of steam when I arrived at the top of the platform steps I went straight to the cab, which was just by the steps, to talk to the driver and his fireman. I loved the trip and savoured every moment knowing full well it might be the last time I would ever be on a footplate, or even see a steam engine on the route. This must have been around 1963/4.

I have come to your title late in the day and so have been buying lots of back issues – sadly, I see my chances of ever reading No 3 are very remote indeed. I have enjoyed every one and am planning, at long last, to create a small, end-to-end model railway featuring a fictitious country terminus; I have started acquiring some rolling stock to this end and have managed to find the complete run of Hornby's beautiful twelve-wheel Pullmans, nearly all of which ran on Southern metals. It is a great time for modelling the Southern Railway.

An image we may have seen before, but especially for Graham Buxton-Smither here is a portable vacuum cleaner. (The sliding door has covered up the 'S.E.' part of the company initials, so it is *not* 'C.R.'. for Caledonian Railway!

I do have a question: have you ever covered the vacuum cleaning wagons used by the SECR, LSWR and eventually the Southern Railway? I'm very curious to know more about them – I've sourced a few images in a couple of books but there's not much information on them. Do you know of a good reference source for details of their interiors and the vacuum cleaning kits that were employed?

Anyhow, I apologise for taking up so much of your time but just wanted to say how much I appreciate the work that you are all doing; long may it continue.'

Graham, thank you indeed. We do receive a few letters of praise but I have always thought it a bit pompous to include every one, although all are of course appreciated. *The Southern Way* was always intended to give those interested in the Southern and of course its constituents a regular 'fix', without we hope repeating too often what had been published elsewhere. Finding a balance is not easy. The obscure and the esoteric, as indeed the vacuum cleaner vans, would fit exactly into the concept and we have tried to cover some of the more unusual topics over the years – and will continue to do so. We have not so far covered your own suggested topic. What we have always tried to do is also point anyone in the appropriate direction, so I might suggest you refer to the late Roger Kidner's excellent work *Service Stock of the Southern Railway* (Oakwood Press, 1980; revised edition 1993), where there is some information and, in the later edition at least, one photo as well.

The following appeared in the *Bournemouth Echo* on Tuesday 28 July 2015:

'A little piece of railway history is gone after the death of a beloved station resident. Hundreds of tributes have flooded in following the passing of the famous Swanage Railway cat. The cat, nicknamed 'Ringwood' by the railway's steam locomotive drivers, firemen, cleaners and shed staff, first arrived at the station approximately six years ago. Staff said she would know the warmest and best places to sleep, occasionally ending up beyond shed limits on an unplanned journey if she was too lazy to wake up. She also proved a hit with visitors and residents of Swanage who visited the station, so much so that tributes and memories of meeting her have now flooded the Swanage Railway's website and Facebook page.

Kevin Potts, from the Swanage Railway, commented: 'Steam locomotive drivers, firemen, cleaners and shed staff at the Swanage Railway have been left saddened as a little piece of railway history passed on. Swanage engine shed was, until Saturday morning, home to Ringwood the shed cat. Sadly, staff arriving as dawn broke found her, not in her usual place curled up next to the shed's coal fire, but lying on the coal dock beside one of the locomotives she inevitably dodged no matter how many times she crossed the tracks daily.'

Kevin added that staff believed Ringwood to have a home elsewhere, but loved the station so much that she returned on a daily basis. Back in the days of steam, most locomotive sheds had their own shed cat. More often than not, the cat chose the shed.

They were working animals, adept at keeping rats and mice at bay in what were some of the last Victorian working conditions left in Britain. In return, the cat would gratefully accept odd items of food from enginemen's rations – either given as a sign of friendship, or snatched behind their backs in an unguarded moment. Some railway sheds even had the cat 'on the books' and the railway company paid a small allowance towards their upkeep. Despite a dangerous environment and staff operating heavy machinery, Swanage's shed cat seemed to love the station anyway. Most railway stations had a shed cat in the past and some still do. When you came back into the crew room after a long day you would more often than not find Ringwood curled up on the clothes you had left out. Railway staff are now thinking of getting a mature cat for the station from a rescue centre, perhaps one that was not suitable for domestic rehoming.'

'Swanage'. RIP.

Next from Chris Sayers-Leavy (Manager of what was left of Ashford railway works, 1990-92.):

'I was a little surprised to read the Editorial of Issue 31 – but I understand your position and trust that you will be able to continue to edit *The Southern Way*. [Chris, your comments are most kind and are appreciated. Several others have also expressed their best wishes and I am similarly grateful. For the present there are no plans to alter the status quo with regard the editorship but longer term any offers would be appreciated!]

I have not yet read through everything in Issue 31, but the picture on page 100 and some of the comments made in the article 'Part 8 From the Southern Railway to the end of the Southern Region' struck a chord with me and I thought that you might like my comments, to use as you see fit.

I was a regular commuter from Broadstairs to various parts of the country via London from 1984 to 2013. The SR units used on this route were generally pretty uninteresting (until the 'Javelins' were introduced), being the original Kent Coast electrification CEP/BEP stock, then Class 375s on the fast (sic) services and VEPs (and latterly downgraded CIGs and BIGs) on the semi fast/stopping services.

Over the years, with the pressure of the developing Medway towns commuter traffic, the supposedly 'fast' domestic services actually got slower and slower to do the 77 miles from London to Broadstairs. The fastest that I ever knew on the route was 1hr 40min, and by the time HS services via Ashford to St Pancras were introduced the original BTR 3 [Boat train route] via Chatham, latterly CTR 3 [Channel Tunnel route] services were taking just under 2 hours to make the journey.

Now, as you know the 'operators' like to tinker with the timetable from year to year, supposedly to make improvements (this depends on your point of view of course!). Anyway, almost in a last fling of 'independent creative thinking' an attempt was made in 1988 to improve the journey time of the fast services from Thanet via BTR 3 by putting an MLV on the front of key services and running them as thirteen-car formations. This did in fact improve matters with a return to timings of about 1hr 45min, and I even saw standing passengers from time to time (who got on at Bromley South when the leading MLV doors were not locked!), decanting at Victoria.

So in the twilight of their years there was an attempt to make use of these MLVs, much under-utilised assets. This of course was commensurate with a pair of MLVs being used to ferry water up to Ramsgate from Dover. This also must have followed the loss of the Royal Mail traffic, as the MLVs had previously been used for dedicated mail services – which in turn were intended to reduce the platform standing times of fast services.

I well recall a week of disruption in the winter of that year, when Thanet was effectively cut off from the rest of Kent by snow! I spent 12 hours on trains one day and did not get any further north than Maidstone East. Having set off on the second London train of the day from Broadstairs, we were reversed at Faversham, then ran to Dover, then up to Ashford – where we thought that we would run via BTR 1 to Bromley (via Chislehurst) but oh no! 'Control' had better ideas … and we were sent up BTR 2 towards Maidstone – only to catch up with the preceding

ex-Thanet service and having to stand in the tunnel. The power was then turned off, which I later found out was due to late-night travellers on a down service who had become gapped and 'snowed in', had had enough and had decided to walk to Maidstone! The end result of this fracas was that we were eventually put together as a twenty-six-coach formation in an attempt to 'charge' up the bank north of Maidstone East station.

Of course the inevitable happened – the whole lot got stuck and, as the driver of our train could not speak to the driver at the very front (despite all the jumpers being connected up, and as there was no gangway on the MLV) he decided to get out and walk forward. To do this he opened his door and climbed down, only to disappear up to his chest in the snow accompanied by a round of applause from all the watching passengers… I'll leave the story at this point as the farce went on and on, culminating later in the day by the passengers effectively 'hijacking' an ECS of Gatwick Mk II stock, destined for Chart Leacon depot, at Ashford (when we eventually got back there) to take us to Ramsgate!

This was also the week , you might recall, that a Class 33 loco with a snowplough on either end got stuck in the snow drifts, and the crew had to be rescued by helicopter!

Re the picture on page 90: just an observation really, based on the caption, but it should of course be remembered that for any transits over the 'open railway' the movement would have required a driver who had 'signed for' the route that was required to be 'inspected' and he would act as a pilotman for the traction concerned, be it a loco or an inspection vehicle. Indeed, if he had also been passed out to drive the vehicle, he would be expected to drive it, rather than just sit there advising the engineers department operator. The upshot of these rules would be that he would deploy an appropriate headcode on the vehicle, and all such vehicles that had to travel on the 'open line' would be provided with a lamp iron as per locos and multiple units for the purpose of displaying the headcodes, either by discs or lamps – i.e. the same rules apply to all forms of traction.

Now some thoughts on rereading Issue 30, 'The Ashford 1948 Wagon Photographs'. Again, just observations really. First, the matter of 'official photographs'. The SR had a well-established photographic section and when I knew of it (in its last few years) it was based in the 'Plan Arches' at Waterloo. Indeed, the whole matter of 'official photographs' goes back to the earliest days of the railways/photography. It was normal, perhaps even customary, for official photographs to have the background of the image 'painted out', and this would involve copy negatives being produced. All negatives would be numbered/identifiable in some way and official prints would be likewise marked. The earliest form of this would be either a 'detail board' being incorporated in the picture (by manufacturers, etc) or by writing in ink on the negative. Right up to BR days this was a well-established process and extensive records were kept. Mike King does not make it clear whether or not it was negatives or prints that were recovered? I suspect it is black & white prints and that these will be stamped on the back with all of the basic information – copyright, date maybe, the location and the negative number. They would normally also be endorsed with whether or not the image could be used for publicity purposes. Without this basic information they are not likely to be 'formal' official photographs and may well be a 'locally organised commission' – but even if this was the case, the photographer is likely to have protected his copyright interests with an address/studio reference and an image number of some kind.'

Chris, the whole issue of copyright of images is a topic that comes up time and time again. Having been involved in well in excess of 100 books over the years I can say that I have only ever been caught out once and that when, having written to the last known address of a well-known photographer, I received no reply, so used the images, credited to him, only to later receive the threat of legal action. The matter was eventually resolved but probably not amicably. The internet of course adds a whole new dimension to the subject. Like many publishers and individuals, I have seen material I own reproduced with no reference or credit – but that is going into a whole new topic.

Most of the official views we use, which clearly are official views, are stamped on the back 'Southern Railway copyright free'. If we get it wrong on official or other images that is not the intention. However, before getting off my soapbox, a comment that I am sure applies to most specialist publishers. The margins in producing books these days for a restrictive audience are getting smaller year on year. If an individual or organisation has an unrealistic opinion of worth it is likely the item will simply not be used.

Chris Sayers-Leavy continues:

'My experience with the Southern Region photographic section was that this was a 'call off' service that any manager could request, the funding being agreed centrally for each department. We used to keep quite detailed departmental records, and the photographic service did likewise and copies of pictures could be ordered up just using the reference number. They had their own 'section policy', which dictated how they worked, but once on site, if it was a local manager's request, the photographer 'worked as required'.

However, they also took commissions for major projects – and they seemed to tackle these as 'free agents' working to an overall brief.

Now on to the way in which the pictures were taken. In my experience; each photographer had his own ideas as to how the composition of the photographs should be arranged, within your requirements, and this may well explain why some pictures were taken from the opposite perspective – it could simply have been a different photographer, particularly if the camera was set up on a tripod and the vehicles were brought 'to the camera'. Alternatively it may have been the location that dictated the orientation of the photograph. The use of tripods would normally be the case, for a good clear and crisp image. A good photographer could also hide a 'multitude of sins' and I have even been on site when pictures were taken in the rain – but from the prints supplied there is no sign of any inclement weather at all. Generally single vehicle pictures standing on S&C or near converging lines have been 'positioned' for the photographer.

A couple of comments on the pictures now. Those on pages 42 and 43 appear to show vehicles very much in their original condition, towards the end of their life, and it is interesting to see that the wheel tyres have been painted white – ready for the pictures to be taken maybe?

The mixture of wheel types is interesting to say the least, with some quite old vehicles being fitted with new one-piece three-hole disc wheels (23682), while others still retain an early split spoke type (fabricated design) – with power braking, surely by this date, these wheels were very much frowned upon for fast running.

Were the self-contained buffers an original fitting on 45682? They look to be something of a retro-fit with the bases being wider than the depth of the headstock.

Lastly, I would suggest that the shunter in the picture on page 47 is actually waiting for the photographer to finish!

I agree that the purpose of the photographs being taken is a curiosity, but it may just be to keep a record of the 'standard' of the work/finish of the vehicles being processed. Having said that, this does not account for some of the pictures not having the background painted out.'

The image of the 10-ton wagon referred to by Chris Sayers-Leavy, complete with a rather bored shunter!

Quiz time

A bit of gentle amusement, with no prizes but the question is 'where and when, and what is going on?'

There is a specific clue in one of the images – why? (It has nothing to do with the engines...)

Answer

I expect 99% of readers will have the answer, but it is the erecting shop at Eastleigh in 1943/44, when twenty-three 2-8-0 locomotives to the Stanier LMS 8F design were built in Hampshire. Ashford also built fourteen and Brighton no fewer than sixty-eight, all in the same period. The specific clue is of course in the second picture where 'S.R.' wagon tarpaulins are hung up against the windows of the works as a blackout precaution.

Southern Railway locomotive No A816
A great engineering venture

No 816 visually at its (her) best when newly converted.

Harry Holcroft MILocoE

Reproduced from the *Stephenson Locomotive Society Journal* No 393, March 1958, with additional comments by Gerry Nichols and Kevin Robertson

Those travelling by train are all familiar with the sight of white clouds of steam rolling across the countryside arising from the exhaust ejected from the chimney of the locomotive, though in this era of superheat it is not so frequently to be seen as in days gone by.

In musing upon these billowing clouds, the thought might occur to some: 'What a waste of steam; if only it could be bottled up and returned to the boiler how great a saving there would be.' My object here is to tell you how this seemingly impossible feat was accomplished, since the present accepted theory on the use of steam in heat engines proves that the work done in compression of a given weight of steam is nearly as great as that given out in its expansion. The accepted efficiency of a railway steam engine at the time was in single-figure percentage points, and low single figures at that. As time passed so improvement was made in exhausts, steam passages, etc. But it would take the work of such visionaries as Chapelon, Porta and Wardale before true advancement was made, although by that time alternative forms of traction had already become established.

It is remarkable that it occasionally happens that some of the most notable advances in science and industry have at times been brought about either by 'outsiders' or by 'rebels' within the ranks. Those taught on orthodox lines are apt to get into a rut by accepting everything without question, but now and again someone comes along who has notions of his own. Such a man was A. P. H. Anderson, at one time a draughtsman in a marine engineering works near Glasgow. His observations led him to think that there were conditions under which exhaust steam might be compressed and so liquified without an excessive expenditure of power. By so doing much heat would be saved by being returned with the feed to the boiler.

Anderson was not by himself in a position to submit his theory to the test, but he found an ally in John McCallum, of Glasgow, who was able to put experimental work in hand on a stationary plant, and a start was made in 1925. After two years of investigation the plant was much simplified and improved, so much so that under optimum conditions it was found that no less than 70% of the heat content of the exhaust steam leaving the engine could be returned to the boiler in the feed before power expenditure in compression rendered a higher return uneconomical.

If exhaust steam at atmospheric pressure is fully condensed by withdrawal of the latent heat, which amounts to 970 British Thermal Units per pound of steam, the resulting hot water can be pumped back to the boiler as feed at or near 212°F with a very small expenditure of power for operating the feed pump.

On the other hand, if exhaust steam is not cooled in any way, it can still be returned as feed if it is compressed to boiler pressure, but the work expended on the steam in doing so would be so great that the net power output of the plant is almost nil, so that the operation is impractical.

The Anderson System takes a mid-course. The exhaust steam is only partially cooled, so that much of the latent heat remains after some 600 BTUs are withdrawn. The resulting steam-water mixture, or 'emulsion' as Anderson termed it, is so handled that it can be compressed and returned as feed with an expenditure of power no greater than that required for the ordinary feed pump, namely no more than 1 to 2 per cent of the power output of the plant. All the 'kick' is taken out of the exhaust steam, and that is the crux of the invention.

Although the scheme originated with an attempt to improve the efficiency of marine engines, it became obvious that the greatest saving was to be effected in those engines exhausting to atmosphere, of which the railway steam locomotive is the most notable example.

In order to exploit the remarkable results obtained on the experimental plant, a move was made to London in 1927 and a number of businessmen in the City were induced to form a company, which was named The Steam Heat Conservation Company, and to supply the capital necessary for development in the expectation of reaping a bountiful harvest in due course.

A demonstration set was arranged at the privately owned Surbiton Electricity Generating Station (Figure 1), where a unit consisting of a water-tube boiler with chain grate stoker and a Belliss & Morcom vertical high-speed engine driving a generator was allocated to the job. The normal condensing apparatus of this set was disconnected and its place taken by a multi-tubular cooler and a compressor. When this was set up and in working order, a number of invitations were circulated to interested parties.

It was open to any visitor to make observations and draw his own conclusions from the result. Those viewing the demonstration could be broadly divided into three groups:

(1) Those who rigidly stood by the teaching of the text books on steam and who would not admit that steam and water could be made to behave in any other manner than that laid down by accepted theory. They honestly believed the whole thing to be fallacious in some way unexplained.

(2) Others who admitted that the results claimed by the inventor were achieved, but they did not accept his explanation of the phenomenon. They thought the result might be due to some fortuitous or unusually favourable arrangement of the plant. In fact they thought it was just a 'fluke'.

(3) The relative few who accepted as true what they saw. They did not necessarily see eye-to-eye with the inventor in his theory, but agreed that a new development in the use of steam had been demonstrated. Some went as far as to declare that the text books on steam would have to be rewritten in the face of this development.

As Technical Assistant to the Chief Mechanical Engineer of the Southern Railway, I was sent by him to investigate the plant at Surbiton and as a result of what I saw my views fell in with those expressed in Group 3. I found that the steam and water circuits were equipped with meters, pressure gauges and thermometers at various points so that it was possible to follow the course and to estimate the flow of steam and the amount of cooling water circulating through the multi-tubular cooler, and by the difference in temperature of the volume flowing to see how much heat was being abstracted thereby from the circuit. By deduction it could be realised that by the amount of heat left in the circuit a considerable saving was being made by the heat return.

My report was to the effect that substantial economy over an engine exhausting to atmosphere and using cold feed was possible by Anderson's system, but that in the case of a railway locomotive the economy attainable in a stationary plant would be offset by the necessity for providing power to operate a draught fan in the absence of a blast pipe and by the variable and somewhat intermittent working of the engine in service, for it was characteristic of Anderson's system that the full

A diagram of the experimental stationary plant at Surbiton Electricity Generating Station.

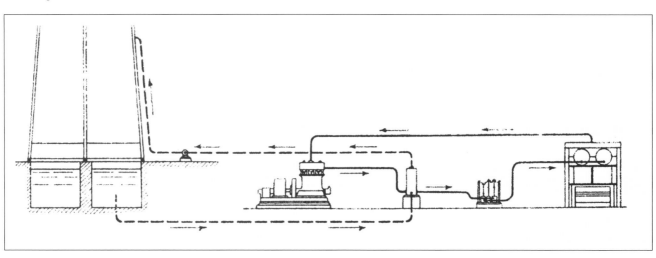

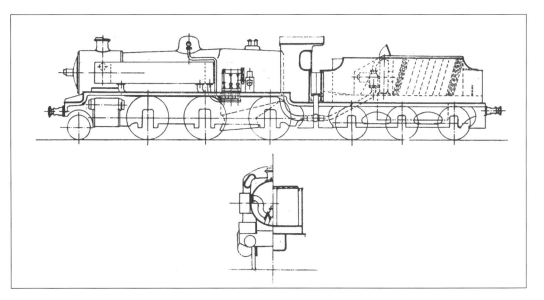

The first proposal for the intended modification. The multi-tubular cooler and compressor are duplicated either side of the framing, not least because of the need to maintain symmetry and weight distribution. Even so, the load of this equipment added an additional 5 tons to the total engine weight. Note the proposed reconstruction of the tender coolers, lined out with its radiators. This also necessitated large-diameter pipe connections between the engine and tender to circulate the cooling water.

economy was not attained until the engine had been working for some time. But even if there was no appreciable saving in fuel, the system would be of benefit in a railway locomotive because the steam would work in a closed circuit and the boiler would be mainly fed with hot and virtually distilled water, the amount of make-up feed being small. This would result in the maintenance of a clean boiler and a great reduction in scale formation and concentration of soluble salts. Boiler washout periods could be extended, so promoting greater availability. Boiler maintenance and repairs would be also minimised by the favourable conditions.

As a result of my report, Mr Maunsell. the CME, called in representatives of the company to see him with a view to considering the application of the Anderson System to a railway locomotive. At the meeting the representatives gave their version as to the explanation of what took place in their handling of the exhaust steam, but Mr Maunsell said he was not concerned in theoretical considerations. If they would arrange for a third party to carry out a test on the Surbiton plant and demonstrate to him an actual saving in fuel consumed in relation to kilowatts recorded at the switchboard by their system as compared with the plant in operation exhausting direct to atmosphere, he would consider the matter further.

The power station engineer agreed to carry out the test, and as a preliminary the generating set concerned was operated with the normal condensing apparatus in use over a period of 48 hours continuous running, during which period the coal supplied to the chain grate stoker was carefully measured and the kilowatts generated were recorded. After this rehearsal the real test began, the condensing gear being disconnected and the exhaust turned to atmosphere. In order that the same power output could be sustained under loss of vacuum, the cut-off of the high-pressure cylinder was increased a little. With these alterations made, another 48-hour test was carried out.

On the completion of this, the Anderson System was brought into use so that the exhaust steam was liquified and returned to the boiler as hot feed, also over a period of 48 hours.

The result of these tests, taking atmospheric working as the basis for comparison, was that the normal system of condensing saved 19% of fuel, while with the Anderson system the saving was no less than 29% over atmospheric working.

When informed of this convincing result, Mr. Maunsell agreed that the company should submit a scheme for the application of the system to a locomotive. As they had no experience of locomotive conditions, my Chief instructed me to collaborate with the firm in order to assist them in producing a practical proposition.

At the first meeting held to outline a scheme it was agreed that a steam-driven fan would have to be provided at the smokebox as a substitute for the normal blast pipe. The apparatus carried on the locomotive, namely the multi-tubular cooler and the compressor, would have to be duplicated and carried on each side of the boiler in order to preserve symmetry and distribute the additional weight evenly. As a substitute for the cooling tower of the stationary plant, the tender would have to be reconstructed to carry a large bank of radiators in conjunction with steam-driven fans and circulating pumps. Large-diameter connections would be necessary between engine and tender to circulate the cooling water (above).

Thus, as in the stationary plant, there were two circuits: in one, the fluid flowed from boiler to cylinders, through a cooler, then by compressor back to boiler. In the other, water flowed to the cooler and returned to radiators, then back through the circulating pump.

It was clear that the attempt to reproduce the layout of the stationary plant on the locomotive involved high first cost and that the scheme would have to be abandoned for something much simpler, and that meant branching out on original lines.

I suggested that the water circulation as a means of extracting heat should be cut out and the air cooling by fans applied directly to the multi-tubular coolers (overleaf), and further that, by introducing with the air a fine spray of water, the capacity for conveying away heat would be greatly increased through the evaporation of the spray carried through the air stream. This proposal enabled the costly provision of a special tender, fitted

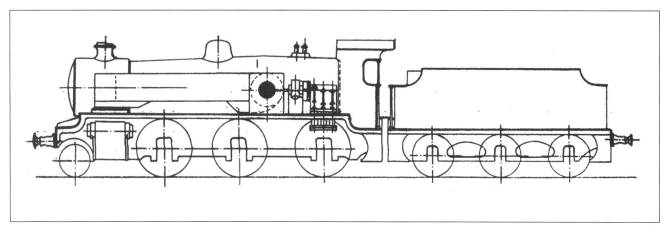

The modification suggested by Holcroft, whereby air cooling by fans applied direct to the multi-tubular coolers was installed. This simplified the design as well as allowing necessary tender exchanges with only minimal modification. (The lack of condensing equipment was also a factor that made a success of the three steam turbine engines then working in Sweden and shortly afterwards on the LMS with No 6202.)

with apparatus, to be dispensed with and some of the steam-driven auxiliaries made unnecessary. Thus the water in the tender became expendable, as in ordinary locomotive working.

Accordingly a special cooler was constructed and tried out on the Surbiton plant. Headers at each end caused the exhaust steam to make three passes through the banks of tubes. A motor-driven fan or impeller forced air carrying with it a spray of cold water over the exterior of the tubes. We were delighted to find that the scheme worked remarkably well, but more water than anticipated had to be used in the spray because some of it did not reach the tubes but passed between them and accumulated in the bottom of the cooler. Thus after some hours' working, the lower tubes became waterlogged, but this condition had no adverse effect on the working. When the fan was eventually stopped, it was discovered that the system continued to operate as well as before, because the exhaust steam in the lowest bank of tubes evaporated the water, and

the spray due to ebullition reached the middle and upper banks, the vapour generated being discharged to atmosphere.

It was then grasped that here was the simple solution. Introduction of air by fans was not called for; all that was necessary was to maintain a depth of about a foot or so of water in the coolers, by introducing a supply direct from the tender to make up for that evaporated and discharged.

Thus in this radical change the water carried in the tender was mainly required for cooling purposes and no longer for feeding the boiler, other than a small amount of make-up for small losses by leakage, etc.

A scheme was then drawn up in 1928 for fitting an engine of the 'N' Class 2-6-0 type (below), This was the most suitable design owing to its outside cylinders and valve gear and medium-sized wheels, so that the apparatus could be carried alongside the boiler on brackets, clear of the coupled wheels. The coolers were placed one on each side of the boiler barrel and the

The scheme as applied to No A816. The additional water supply from the tender was direct to the coolers either side of the framing where a depth of approximately 1 foot of water was maintained. (From Holcroft's drawing and indeed from a study of the photographs it will be noted that the coolers are placed on the framing at a higher level than that of the tender water tank. How the requisite level in the coolers was therefore maintained should the water level in the tender be low is not certain. Presumably a non-return valve and pump may have been involved.)

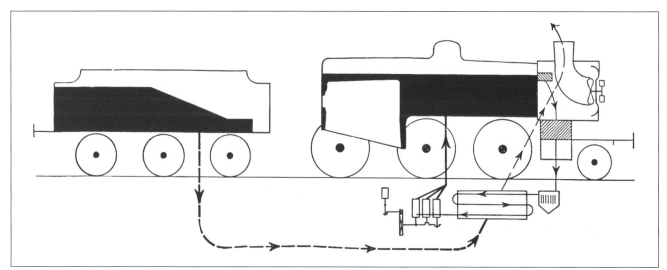

compressors with their small vertical steam engines were on each side of the firebox. The fan for the induced draught was directly driven by a rotary steam engine of Anderson's design in which four cylinders, arranged radially, all drove on a single crank, cut-off being fixed at 25 per cent. This was fixed on the smokebox door of special design and drew in gases from the smokebox and, after reversal of direction by a shrouding, discharged them through an uptake in the shape of a large right-angle bend attached to the base of the chimney. The normal blast pipe was retained and its orifice projected into the uptake at the bend, so that it could function in the normal way when desired. A butterfly valve was fitted just below the orifice so that the blast pipe could be closed and so bring the Anderson System into use.

Exhaust steam from the base of the blast pipe was conveyed by pipes through the sides of the smokebox where grease separators were located. Pipe connections from these carried the exhaust to the multi-tubular coolers. A safety valve was provided on each header, set at 10lb per sq in.

At the bottom of the rear header of the cooler the partly condensed steam, much reduced in volume but greatly increased in density, was conveyed to the compressor, and from there by the usual feed pipe to the clack box on the side of the dome.

Small rotary pumps of the gear type were driven off the compressors to supply feed water to the coolers.

The stipulation was that the railway put aside a locomotive for the company to try out its plant, the agreement being that the SHC Co should provide the main pieces of the apparatus; the railway would on its part provide the brackets to carry it and do all the pipework and rodding, together with special chimney, uptake, blast pipe and smokebox door, and do all the erecting.

Drawings of the apparatus were duly submitted, approved by the CME and a grant obtained through the General Manager to cover the cost of the experiment.

An order was placed on Eastleigh Works early in 1930 and the drawing office got busy with the actual arrangement and detail drawings. When all the parts had been made and it was possible to arrange a date for assembly, locomotive No A816 was selected as it had a low mileage after general repairs and had been well run in. Subsequently it was thought advisable to change the boiler for another that would not be likely to require repairs for a long time to come.

The engine was turned out of the erecting shop in September 1930, and I went to Eastleigh to take part in the initial run up and down the length of the Works sidings. When steam was raised, the first thing we did was to try the induced draught. On opening the steam valve, the fan started up and there was a fierce back draught at the firehole and all the cinders and ash were blown out of the ash pan in a cloud of dust. Due to a misunderstanding between the makers of the rotary engine and the makers of the fan, the fan blades had been made to the wrong hand and so exerted pressure instead of vacuum in the smokebox (below and overleaf).

Below and overleaf: **The engine in its modified state at Eastleigh and almost complete. Externally it will be noted that the sides are lined out, so presumably the complete engine was painted in suitably adapted Southern livery. From an engineering perspective these two views are of specific interest. Notice that the angle of the fan blades changes between the two views, which ties in exactly with Holcroft's comment that they had originally been fitted the wrong way round. On the basis of the soot present in the head-on view, it is reasonable to state that the interior works view of the engine has the blades incorrectly fixed and the head-on image is in its modified form.**

However, with the induced draught shut off, the engine was tried up and down the yard with the blower slightly on to raise steam. After the engine had worked with the blast pipe open and with the set on one side at work so as to eliminate air mixed with the steam, I pulled the rod operating the butterfly valve in the blast pipe so as to close it. The engine then ran without any exhaust to atmosphere and we anxiously watched the back pressure gauge, but the needle remained at zero and scarcely flickered during a number of trips. This was satisfactory as far as it went, but the engine had to be laid aside for some weeks while a new impeller with blades to the reverse hand was obtained from the makers. The replacement turned out to be inefficient and another firm had to be found to supply something better. All this involved a delay of two months.

The photo giving a side view of the engine (below left) as originally turned out shows the exhaust pipe emerging from the smokebox and connecting to the grease separator, and this in turn to the front header of the cooler. Here, the relief valve is also seen. The outlet from the rear header connects to the compressor by a much smaller pipe than the inlet, due to large decrease in volume and increase in density. The three-throw compressor is driven through gearing by a single-cylinder vertical donkey engine. As this was not always self-starting, a barring gear was carried through into the cab in order to turn it over a dead centre.

The gear pump and its connections can be seen and also the delivery pipe to the clack box on the dome. The second clack box is for injector delivery of make-up feed water. The exhausts from the fan engine and compressor engine are taken to the separator and so recovered with the main steam.

The front view (below right) shows the smokebox door closed and its pipe connections to the fan engine within, steam and exhaust being led through trunnions in line with the door hinges, so that the smokebox could be opened without breaking any pipe connections. This arrangement worked very well.

The vapour generated in the coolers is seen to be led by pipes to discharge at each side of the chimney top and so carried away with the smokebox gases.

Below left: **No A816 seen side-on with its ancillary 'plumbing'. (Eight official views of No A816 in its experimental guise appear in the Eastleigh photographic register. Six are undated and follow in sequence, possibly implying that they were taken during or when the modifications were complete, and one last one is recorded from 27 March 1936. This latter date contradicts Holcroft slightly as by implication he infers that the trials ceased in 1934. It seems unlikely that the Southern Railway would be prepared to allow the engine to remain stored for any longer than was necessary before restoring it to normal use.)**

With the engine ready for running, my part in affairs ended with the handing over to the CME's Testing Section for trials, though I made trips on the footplate from time to time to keep in close touch with results.

The method of operation was to start up one of the compressors while the engine was standing with the donkey engine running at about 75rpm and to pump in about 8 inches of water into the cooler. This preliminary cleared away any condensation and warmed up the apparatus.

On starting away with a train, the engine was allowed to exhaust to atmosphere for a short time to clear out air from the system, while the donkey engine was speeded up to 600rpm. When the valve in the blast pipe was closed, a back pressure of some 5lb per sq in was normally set up and the exhaust was returned to the boiler as condensate.

If the load was heavy, the second set was brought into use, one set being capable of handing about two-thirds of the full output of the locomotive.

The reason for the back pressure, which is equivalent to that set up by the contracted orifice of the blast pipe, is that a temperature head has to be brought about in the cooler so that the heat transfer through the tube walls can be effected, the inner surface being at about 230°F while the outer surface under atmospheric pressure is 212°. Hence the thermal head is about 18°F.

In the stationary plant under continuous working only about 4lb back pressure is necessary, but in a locomotive the steam is not pure but is contaminated by a small percentage of air, hence the higher back pressure.

In practice, these back pressures were sometimes excessive, reaching the 10lb at which the relief valves were set. This indicated a larger percentage of air present in the steam.

Air enters the boiler in the injector feed, being dissolved in the raw water and also entrained by the injector. Apart from that, air enters the exhaust system every time the regulator is closed, by the pumping action of the cylinders. As much as possible of this contamination of the steam has to be got rid of by exhausting to atmosphere before the Anderson System can work properly.

The effect of air, or other permanent gas, present in the steam is twofold: it lowers the temperature at which condensation occurs and conversely raises the pressure

Below right: **With the smokebox door closed, the pipe connections are seen. The two pipes feeding into the chimney either side of the rim carry vapour generated in the coolers. The pipe connections to the fan engine are also visible.**

necessary to create the 18°F thermal head. A secondary effect is due to the release of air on the tube surface as the steam condenses, so acting as an insulator to impede the heat flow to the cooling water.

There were times when high back pressure persisted in the trials of the locomotive, which no amount of venting seemed to reduce. This was attributed to slugs of greasy water being carried through the exhaust system when starting from cold. Should these overwhelm the grease separators, the inner surface of the tubes would be coated with a non-conducting film and it took a long time to get the surfaces scrubbed clean by the passage of exhaust steam over them.

Another trouble experienced was due to the collection of ash and cinders in the blast pipe above the butterfly valve after the fan had been at work. If this valve was opened, the collection dropped down the blast pipe if the regulator was shut and no exhaust steam issuing. As a result, grit worked through the apparatus and got on the seats of the compressor valves, so putting the compressors out of action.

On another occasion the system failed to function after the engine had been standing in the Works Sidings for some weeks awaiting replacements for parts of the apparatus. The usual remedies failed and it was ultimately discovered that the tubes in the cooler were pitted through with pin-holes, due to water having been inadvertently left in. The concentration of salts due to evaporation had made it highly corrosive, and re-tubing became necessary.

Apart from these operational teething troubles, there were many others of a mechanical nature, which will be evident in the description of the trials that follows here.

To return to the trials on the road, it will be remembered that the original fan was to the wrong hand. The replacement, secured after a two-month delay, created a vacuum in the smokebox of 5 inches of water gauge but, in running in, the pistons of the rotary engine gave trouble and had to be returned to the makers due to deficient lubrication. It was therefore not until mid-February 1931 that the first trial run was made. The engine ran light on the Romsey branch, a load being obtained by screwing on the tender hand brake for periods. On this occasion one of the donkey engines ran hot due to some failure of the forced lubrication. The chain drive between donkey engines and compressors was unsatisfactory, so it was decided to substitute gear wheels (below).

The next run was not until the end of April. This was on the Romsey branch and on this occasion, at which I was present, a gear pump broke down and the valves of the compressors broke. These breakdowns were attributed to unrestricted speed of revolution and it was decided to fit the donkey engines with governors.

Due to the time taken to execute the necessary repairs and alterations, it was not until mid-June that the engine was on the road again. I was present at the trial run to Micheldever on the main line. With lighter valve springs the compressors ran well and the back pressure due to exhaust was down to

A newly discovered view 'snapped' outside the front of Eastleigh Works. Considering the number of runs documented by Holcroft – and presumably those also carried out under the auspices of the Testing Section – it is a pity that no views of the engine actually working a train have so far been discovered, unless of course you know different… At first glance the engine appears to be in steam but on closer examination the smoke is emanating from a pipe attached to the brickwork. It is likely the engine was located here either awaiting or having returned from a trial – notice the open door behind. Certainly in later years, the trials involving No 36001 were carried out with the engine based at the nearby running shed, but the Works also had a test crew who would take a newly repaired engine on a test run before it was passed to the adjacent running shed.

5lb per sq in, but there was a persistent and unpleasant water hammer in the delivery pipes to the clack boxes.

Investigation followed and another run was made on 9 July to Basingstoke. The left-hand side broke down, but the right-hand gave good results. Against the 1 in 250 gradient and with tender hand-brake screwed on hard, the fan maintained boiler pressure against full regulator and a 30 per cent cut-off.

Repairs having been carried out, a short run was made to Dunbridge on the Romsey branch and as a result it was arranged to make the next test run by double-heading the van train from Eastleigh to Basingstoke.

This took place on 31 July 1931. The train was composed of vacuum-fitted stock, there being thirty-three vehicles comprising vans of various sorts and empty passenger coaches. It was drawn by No E445, 'T14' Class, and No. A816 piloted the train. The driver of the former was instructed to crack open his regulator only far enough to keep the sight feed lubricator at work and to leave the pulling to the trial engine.

The result was a dismal failure, for No A816 had to be taken off at Winchester with the pressure down to 125lb and a large loss of water level.

The company was not satisfied with its compressors and decided to replace them with others of simpler design (opposite) and with a larger fall in level between cooler outlet and compressor inlet in order to increase the head.

It was the end of August before these were in place, and a run to Micheldever showed a great improvement, but the fan was not satisfactory. It should be explained that in the first instance a reducing valve was fitted in the steam supply to the fan to restrict maximum pressure to 160lb. This gave a margin of 40lb below the maximum boiler pressure of 200lb so that fan speed would not fall off with a decreasing boiler pressure and give a constant 1,000rpm or so. As this failed to produce sufficient smokebox vacuum, the reducing valve was taken off in order to get some 1,500rpm with 200lb pressure. The snag here was that falling boiler pressure resulted in falling fan speed and matters would go from bad to worse unless the regulator was eased.

The higher speed of revolution led to overstressing of the parts of the rotary engine and failures were apt to occur from fatigue fractures. The company therefore decided to interpose a 2-to-1 gear between engine and fan, but in order to preserve the axial relationship this had to be of the sun-and-planet type. To compensate for loss of power due to lower engine speed, cut-off had to be increased from 25 to 33 per cent., making the fan less economical.

It was Armistice Day, 11 November, when a second run was made with the van train to Basingstoke. I was present this time, and just as the engine was leaving the yard a lubricating pipe on the right-hand donkey put that set out of action. Instead of cancelling the trip, it was agreed to carry on and do the best possible with the left-hand side in action. The result with improved compressors and geared fan was a veritable triumph.

The train consisted of twenty-two vacuum-braked vans and coaches totalling 142 wheels and was drawn by a 'T14' Class engine, thereby repeating conditions as for the first trial. The

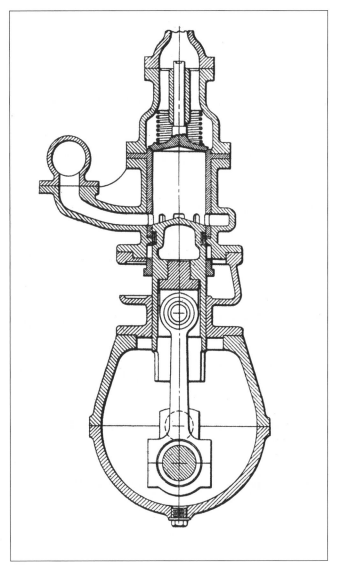

A drawing of the revised compressor fitted.

20-mile-long gradient of 1 in 252 to the Litchfield summit was covered in 45 minutes with the regulator full open and the reverser in Notch 2¼. In the ordinary way this would have created much noise and clouds of steam, but with the condensing set in action it was all absorbed with the ease with which snow would melt in a furnace! The engine was as silent as an electric locomotive and the only faint noises were due to slight pounding of the rods and a small blow at a piston gland. This had to be experienced to be believed; but for the regulator being wide open and the reverser well over one would have imagined that the second engine was propelling the first.

The miscellaneous lot of stock necessitated a large amount of steam for the small ejector to make good the vacuum, due to leakage. These odd vehicles are not maintained at the standard reached in regular passenger trains, hence there was a loss of boiler water that had to be restored by use of the injector. The fan maintained the boiler pressure at 180 to 190lb, but introduction of cold feed pulled this down to 170lb on one or two occasions for a minute or so.

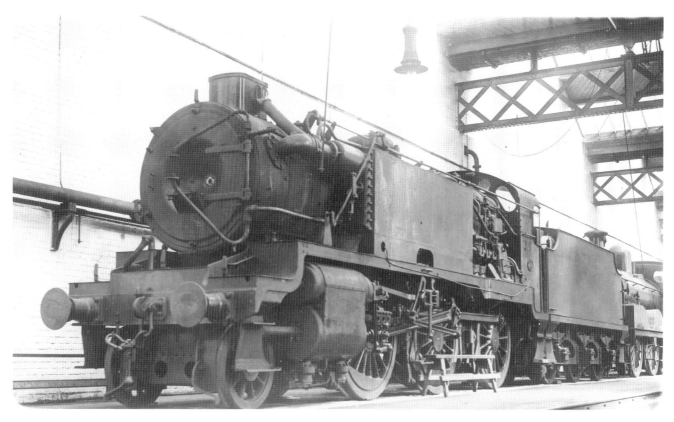

No A816 in the Paint Shop, seemingly stored and likely awaiting a decision with the project abandoned. A number of changes appear to have been made to the original locomotive as originally seen, including the shape of the chimney and pipework leading to the smokebox fan. The engine also appears somewhat 'travel weary'.

The Test Engineer was so pleased with the working that he decided to carry on to Woking, where the train was broken up, and to run on light to Nine Elms in order to start his coal and water consumption tests from the London end.

However, the engine failed to reproduce quite such good form and was therefore returned to Eastleigh pending the next step to be taken.

The position then was that the earlier mechanical troubles had been overcome and some experience gained in the working of the system, but there was insufficient induced draught for full loads. However, enough confidence had been established for the engine to run alone with a train of empty passenger stock, and trials then began between Eastleigh and Bournemouth Central and back.

Early in December I managed to scramble aboard the train as it was leaving Eastleigh, but returned on the footplate from Bournemouth to Southampton, a run just short of 30 miles and covered in about 40 minutes, the load being some 180 tons. Everything went without a hitch and there was only a small loss of water level, due to the use of the small ejector. A signal check approaching Redbridge caused the closing of the regulator and the injector was only applied then in the normal way to prevent blowing off.

This performance was all very well as far as it went, but it seemed to me that there was little point in working at half power and that it was useless to continue until there had been a solution to the draught question so that the engine could work the same loads as the normal 'N' Class engines. So from the beginning of 1932 I ceased to take any active part, though trials continued in desultory fashion for another two years before they were ended, the apparatus removed and the engine returned to normal duties (above).

A De Laval geared turbine was substituted for the rotary engine of the fan, but it proved much too extravagant in steam consumption. A reversion was made to the original condition, but a breakdown of the fan occurred on its second trip.

Early in 1933 an attempt was made to utilise the vapour issuing from the coolers to create blast in the base of the chimney in place of the fan. As anticipated, it proved to be a complete wash-out.

The company was given a further extension of time to produce a solution to the draught question, but it failed to do so and the experiment just fizzled out.

As far as the affairs of the Steam Heat Conservation Company were concerned, the change-over of electricity supply to Surbiton from DC to AC caused the dismantling of the power station and with it the demonstration set. In its place a small layout was installed in a railway arch at Bermondsey, South London, consisting of a vertical gas-fired boiler, engine and generator and a water rheostat, as well as cooler and compressor.

The procedure here was to raise steam and generate current, adjusting the rheostat until steady running was attained with the engine exhausting to atmosphere. The gas

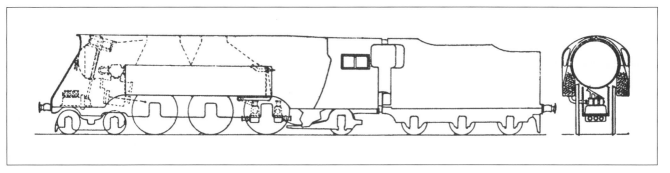

The initial plan for the incorporation of the condensing equipment in a member of the 'Merchant Navy' Class. With the coolers included under the casing this might have affected their efficiency in addition to creating difficulties with access and of course adding a further 5 tons to the weight of the engine.

consumption to boiler was then recorded against kilowatts generated over a period. Change-over would then be made to the system, the exhaust being closed and the cooler and compressor brought into action. As this began to take effect, pressure in the boiler blew off at the safety valve and the gas consumption was progressively reduced as this occurred from time to time until steady conditions were established. Gas consumption was again recorded over a period and showed a marked reduction in relation to kilowatts.

Some colliery companies in the North of England gave a trial to the system on their winding engines, but the working was too intermittent to show much economy.

In the later stages Lord Moyne took over the Chairmanship of the company, but he was subsequently appointed High Commissioner in Egypt, only to be assassinated in Cairo. Anderson, the inventor, died in 1938, a disappointed man, and on the outbreak of war in 1939 the company was dissolved and the patents allowed to lapse. A direct hit by a bomb destroyed its former office in Victoria Street in 1941, and with it what records and drawings that were there. I met the company's former consulting engineer after this happening, and he told me of the deaths of all others involved and the melancholy ending of this great adventure, saying, 'It's all yours now,' meaning that with the knowledge and experience I had gained I was free to exploit the system. He in turn died in 1947, so that I am the only survivor left to tell the whole story.

There is, however, a sequel to this story that you may like to hear about. Mr Bulleid had succeeded Mr Maunsell in 1937 and in a conversation he had with me during the War on the subject of locomotive developments, he raised the question of condensing on locomotives. I then told him of the experiments made with No A816, no details of which had been published because it was hoped to make a fresh start at some future time. Mr Bulleid was greatly interested and had all the papers and records turned up. After studying them, he came to the conclusion that the scheme was quite practical, given a solution of the induced draught question. With the great advances that had since been made in aerodynamics, he thought that a second attempt would have a better chance of success. He therefore instructed me to prepare a scheme to make a new start after the War, taking in the lessons and experiences gained at the first attempt.

The drawing above shows the proposal outline for an engine of the 'Merchant Navy' Class, and I have Mr Bulleid's permission to disclose the plan. It shows a fan and its casing mounted on top of the smokebox in place of the normal chimney; this is driven by a small enclosed high-speed engine mounted on the framing at the front end through a bevel gear box having a ratio of about 3 to 1 and a shaft making about 60° with the horizontal. The steam would be taken from the main steam pipe to the cylinders so that the fan starts to operate on opening of the regulator. There would, however, be an overriding hand control for the fireman to regulate the speed, and a non-return valve below it would allow a small amount of live steam to be supplied to keep the fan revolving when the regulator was closed and so take the place of the normal blower.

The easy sweep of the smokebox gases to the fan will be noted, and also the absence of a blast pipe, so giving the minimum of obstruction in access to tubes and superheater elements, other than the shaft. It was intended to make this hollow for lightness and with splined ends so that it could be drawn up through the centre of the self-contained fan, after the fashion of a half-shaft in the back axle of a motor vehicle. Inside the smokebox it was planned to protect the shaft by a heat-insulated casing open to atmosphere at its lower end, so that cold air could be drawn up inside and outside the shaft in order to keep the ball bearings of the fan at a safe temperature.

By partially lifting the shaft, the middle piston and piston valve could be withdrawn, and by removing the shaft altogether its casing could then be taken out, so leaving a clear smokebox for work on tubes or elements.

This layout of apparatus provides for very robust and reliable construction, and a very moderate speed of revolution of the engine would through the gear give adequate fan speed. Smokebox gases pass direct to the fan with the minimum of loss as compared with the tortuous path of gases in the case of No A816.

The fan and its motor being independent of one another takes care of any slight misalignment due to thermal expansion or other causes.

The coolers are shown tucked away under the streamlined casing and moulded to its contour, discharge of vapour being made on top of the boiler barrel well above the cab windows.

The pair of self-driven compressors are located between the frames, one on each side of the trailing coupled axle and well below the level of the cooler outlets.

In order to minimise losses of boiler water and the compensating introduction of raw make-up feed water, it was intended to provide a mechanical exhauster as used on diesel and electric locomotives for maintaining the vacuum brake, using the small ejector only in emergency. Loss of steam at pop safety valves would have been minimised by the provision of a small pilot valve set to blow off in advance of the main valves and so give warning to the enginemen. The question of steam heating of the train might have been overcome through the provision of a monotube steam generator inserted in one or more flue tubes in the boiler barrel.

It may well be asked what were the advantages resulting from this scheme. In the first place, the apparatus would weigh little or no more than some feed water heating systems and be no more complicated. Instead of recovering some 10 per cent of steam from cylinders, the system returns 100 per cent.

In operation, the scheme outlined offered many advantages beyond the saving of fuel and water. Higher acceleration of a train from rest or recovery from checks is possible because the fan automatically starts up on the opening of the regulator and gives full boiler power straight away. There are no heavy exhaust beats to disturb the fire, so tractive effort is only limited by the adhesion available.

More power is available at speed because there is a greater evaporation of water per pound of coal fired; alternatively, there is a secondary fuel saving due to lowered rate of combustion per square foot of grate for an equal evaporation when not using the system. Spark-throwing is reduced, the size and amount of particles being smaller on account of the non-pulsating draught. Finally, there is suppression of noise, being no more than that given out by an electric locomotive.

As regards the tender, its virtual capacity is extended due to lower coal and water consumption, resulting in its running longer distances between fillings.

From the maintenance point of view, the working in a closed circuit results in a clean boiler, the impurities from the small amount of make-up feed being the only consideration. Therefore, wash-out periods would be extended, repairs reduced and a larger mileage obtained between shoppings.

While the oil separators do not remove the whole of the cylinder oil from the feed, previous experience shows that there is no appreciable accumulation in the boiler. In any case, mineral oil is only harmful if it comes in contact with the heating surfaces and coats them; precautions can be taken to avoid this, for it was the practice at wash-out in the original trial to fill up the boiler before lowering the level, and to allow water to overflow at the highest point, so displacing any oil floating on the surface, after which the boiler could be safely emptied.

All precipitation of impurities in raw water and concentration of soluble salts takes place in the coolers. The soluble salts can be rejected with any matter in the form of sludge at the end of each journey by the mere opening of a discharge cock. As the temperature does not rise above 212°F, no hard deposits are

formed on the tubes and any soft coating can be removed by hosing down through wash-out plug holes. This work can be quickly done between turns of duty, as it involves no cooling down, so there is no loss of availability from this operation.

The abolition of the blast pipe isolates the exhaust system from contact with smokebox gases and dust (as occurs when drifting with the regulator shut). The result is that carbonisation and fouling of piston heads, steam passages and piston valves is largely obviated, so that a clean engine results. Decomposition of oil on the hot surfaces in the presence of air is avoided by the maintenance of a steamy volume through the exhausts from fan and compressor ticking over after the regulator is shut.

The result of all this is that wear of rings and surfaces is reduced and the amount of de-carbonisation in sheds at piston and valve examinations is minimised. Greater mileages between shoppings are, therefore, to be expected and greater availability at sheds.

Bearing in mind the experience with No A816, it was not intended to launch this scheme without careful preparatory work, so that immediate success could be looked for in service. The drawing below shows a boiler of the 'Merchant Navy' Class fixed as a stationary with a firing platform, a calibrating water tank equipped with an 11mm injector, and a supply of weighed fuel. A temporary smokebox containing a fan driven by an electric motor is provided for creating the draught, and there is an expansion chamber and silencer for receiving boiler steam regulated through a gate valve.

From this set-up, data would have been obtained as to vacuum, temperature and volumes of smokebox gas in relation to the evaporation of given quantities of water and coal consumed in doing so at ¼, ½, ¾ and full load. From this it would have been possible to design the necessary draughting arrangement for the locomotive.

Simultaneously with this test, it was intended to install a small plant to test the Anderson System (opposite top). This would have consisted of a gas-fired vertical boiler, expansion chamber, cooler, compressor driven by an electric motor, and all the necessary flow meters, gauges and thermometers to ascertain what was taking place in the system and so proportion the full-scale apparatus to give optimum results.

The bottom image opposite shows the smokebox and its draught apparatus as it would have been designed from data obtained; also one set of the full-scale apparatus connected up for trial on the ground. Should this have proved satisfactory in all respects, it would have been subjected to a reliability trial lasting several days. Given a successful issue, the fitting up of the locomotive could then have proceeded with a good prospect of getting away without any serious teething troubles.

The plan for a test rig involving a 'Merchant Nay' boiler. In the event this was not built.

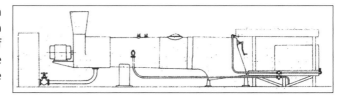

At the same time as the boiler test rig, the plan was also to install a small test plant. Again this was not constructed.

None of these proposals for trials with a 'Merchant Navy' boiler is dated and it is difficult to gauge accurately a timescale when they might have been drawn and/or proposed. The early days of the Second World War are unlikely, possibly some time from 1944 onwards, but likely to have been before the 1945 General Election, with the incoming Socialist Government and its avowed intent to nationalise the railways. Could this be a side of Mr Bulleid that we have not considered in the past, a man of caution, content to develop and test his ideas thoroughly before committing to full-scale production? Had he even been privately prepared to admit that caution was the 'watchword'? We may quickly dismiss this notion, as 70-plus 'Light Pacifics' were ordered straight off the drawing board to the same basis design (and with similar foibles) to the larger 'MN' type. It cannot be later than 1947 either, for with the end of the Southern Railway as a separate organisation he would surely have wished to hurry through any experimentation, as indeed was the case with 'Leader', thus presenting the newly nationalised organisation with a fait accompli. More likely these plans were little more than just an idea with probably both Bulleid and Holcroft knowing that there was no chance of them progressing.

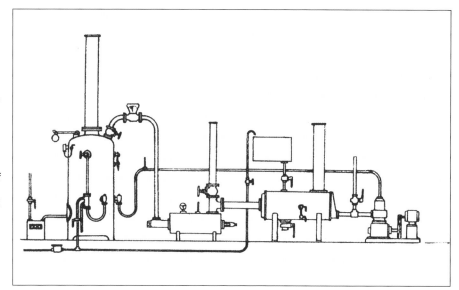

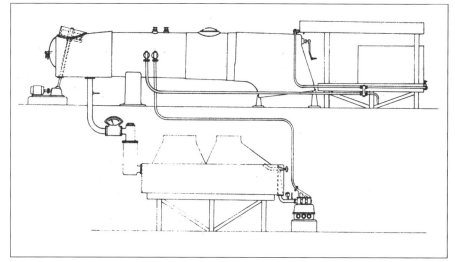

It was intended that this development would have followed on from the 'Leader' Class, but unfortunately the railways were nationalised before any preliminary steps could be taken and the new regime was not interested in anything but the creation of a series of standard types of locomotives of general utility. I have Mr Bulleid's authority for saying that it was his intention to revive the experiment at Inchicore Works, Dublin, when he joined the CIE but that, owing to the heavy dieselisation programme, he has not had staff available to do anything in the matter.

In conclusion, it might be mentioned that beyond the plan for the 'Merchant Navy' Class engine described, Mr Bulleid thought that the ultimate stage for future consideration would be the recovery of the vapour boiled off in the coolers. Not only would it save a lot of water, but the condensate would be pure, so avoiding the feeding of raw water to the coolers. The scheme that I outlined to meet this needed a special eight-wheeled tender to carry cooling fans and radiator grids to condense the vapour (overleaf). It was proposed to install an exhaust steam turbine on the tender to operate under a low vacuum and to drive an electric generator. Current would be supplied from this to motors for driving the cooling fans and the compressors and draught fan on the locomotive. Thus heat units in the vapour would be turned to good use and so save the need for supplying boiler steam to the auxiliaries, in which case the full 30 per cent saving in fuel, realised in stationary plants, would become feasible on long runs.

Whether the saving in cost of coal and water would be sufficient to offset the additional first cost and complication of the special tender is problematical under normal locomotive working. It would, however, offer a cheaper and simpler alternative to the condensing locomotives, such as those developed in Germany during the War and now used on certain lines of the South African Railways.

I have introduced these later developments arising from the experience with No A816 to indicate the 'might-have-been' and, by contrast, to point to the doldrums into which steam locomotive design has entered and the tame acceptance that nothing further can be done to improve thermal and operational efficiency.

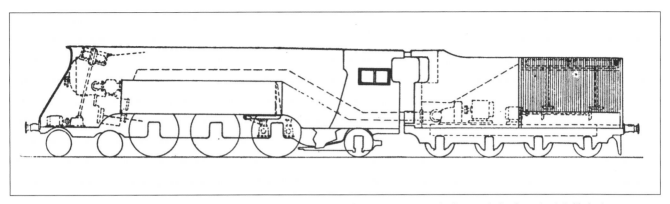

Harry Holcroft's ultimate development with vapour recovery included. With the limited opportunity for long periods of running it is likely that any benefits obtained would have been negated by the complexities involved. This would be the same fate as many other steam experiments, marginal improvement to be measured against the practical inability to run a train at constant speed – unlike the operation of the condensing equipment (or a turbine) when in a stationary environment. We should applaud Messrs Maunsell and Holcroft for their initial attempts but, as with so much in the way of steam experimentation, outside circumstances totally beyond the control of engineers would prevail to prevent further development.

SR 2-6-0 'N' Class engine No A816

Cylinders (2)	19' x 28'
Coupled wheel diameter	5ft 6in
Boiler heating surface	173sq ft
Tubes and 21 flues	1,390.6sq ft
Firebox 135.0sq ft	
Total Evaporative 1525.6 sq. ft.	
Superheater	285.0sq ft
Grate area	25.0sq ft
Working pressure	200lb per sq in
Weight in working order:	
Normal engine of class	61 tons 4cwt
Weight of two condensing sets, induced draught, piping and rods	5 tons
Total weight of engine No A816	66 tons 4cwt
Tender water capacity	3,500 gallons
Tender coal capacity	5 tons
Tender weight	40 tons 10cwt
Cooler	435 tubes of ¾in outside diameter, 10ft 7½in long, 867sq ft cooling surface
Exhaust steam inlet	6in diameter
Outlet to compressor	2½in diameter
Compressor	three single-acting cylinders, 4½in diameter by 6in stroke, 120rpm
Donkey engine	single cylinder, double-acting, 5in diameter by 4in stroke, fixed cut-off 30%, 600rpm, geared 5 to 1 to compressor
Induced draught	Fan of 2ft 7in diameter, 1,000rpm (normal)
Fan engine	Radial type with anchored piston rods, four single-acting cylinders, fixed cut-off 25%, 1,000rpm (normal), 1,500rpm (max), 50rpm (idling)

The Southern Railway engine building programme, 1931-40

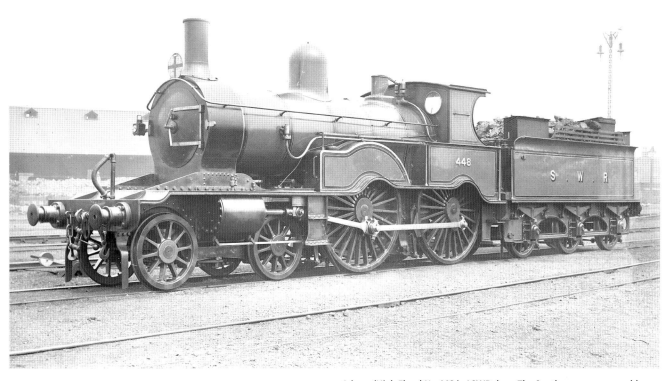

Adams 'High Flyer' No 448 in LSWR days. The Southern was reasonably well off with engines of the 4-4-0 type, although a cull of all sixty-eight of the remaining Adams type was planned. This particular example had been withdrawn some years earlier but the style would continue to be represented by odd members of the 'X2', 'T3' and 'T6' types, which would continue in service (on paper at least) until the 1940s.

Gerry Nichols

The late Sid Nash is well known as a railway photographer and recorder, particularly of the railway scene in and around Eastbourne from the late 1930s to his death in 2004 at the age of 83. His working life was spent on the Southern and British Railways in the Traffic Department. He was a great collector of railway ephemera and left his negatives and papers to the Stephenson Locomotive Society – the Weekly Notices took up about two-thirds of a Transit van, and were mostly disposed of through the late Mike Higson! Having succeeded to the responsibility of SLS Librarian, I am relieved not to have to preserve so much fragile acid paper from disintegration!

One item that Sid 'rescued' is a red ledger with the title of this article. On the first page it has a note: 'Engines which should be provided for Traffic if Engineering Restrictions removed'. Under 'Proposed Revised Building and Scrapping Programme', each class is addressed at each depot against:

A BOOKED DUTIES based on Summer Workings 1930 (Saturday 2 August less 29 deducted for Brighton Electrification)

B SPECIAL DUTIES based on Saturday 2 August 1930 plus 24 small class engines for Fruit, Race, etc, traffic

C ENGINES UNDER REPAIRS AT DEPOTS based on Saturday 2 August 1930

D ENGINES IN (OR AWAITING ACCEPTANCE IN) SHOPS based on Saturday 2 August 1930

E ENGINES SPARE AT DEPOTS for washing out and other requirements

Also in the book is a loose-leaf list of allocations of locomotives to Central Division depots and the ex-LBSC locomotives on other divisions dated 4 April 1929. Table 1 gives an interesting comparison of the pre-Brighton electrification situation. Brighton shed takes the biggest hit of twenty-five, followed by Three Bridges losing four locos (Ardingly and Horsted Keynes), and West Croydon eight locos covering main-line suburban duties. It will be noted that this exceeds the twenty-nine locomotives in the definition of Category A, which is presumably a Traffic-oriented conservatism.

Table 1 Allocations before and after the Brighton electrification situation

Allocation	Battersea Park	New Cross Gate	West Croydon	Tunbridge Wells	West Horsham	Three Little Bridges	Hampton	Bognor	Brighton	Newhaven	Eastbourne	St Leonards	Fratton LBSC
4 April 1929	76	99	20	22	33	26	11	17	133	20	45	16	30
1931-40 from Building Programme	76	91	12	24	33	22	7	22	108	20	46	35	19

Southern Railway rolling stock 1930-31

The SLS *Journal* of 1931, page 78, summarises Southern Railway locomotive stock for January 1931 compared to the status on 1 January 1930, as in Table 2; it will be noted that it excludes locomotives on the Isle of Wight. The reduction of one 'A1X' and two 'O2' locos was the result of the transfer of No B650 to become W9 and Nos E208 and E220 to become W17 and W18.

Table 2 Southern Railway locomotive stock, 1 January 1931 and 1 January 1930

Eastern	1.1.31	1.1.30	Central	1.1.31	1.1.30	Western	1.1.31	1.1.30
751	1	1	A1X	9	10	0298	3	3
B	1	1	B1	3	8	0330	5	9
B1	27	27	B2X	9	20	0395	20	20
B2	4	4	B4	21	21	0415	2	2
C	108	108	B4X	12	12	0458	2	2
D	30	30	C2	14	14	700	30	30
D1	21	21	C2X	41	41	735	1	1
E	15	15	C3	10	10	A12	68	71
E1	11	11	D1	10	10	B4	25	25
F	0	7	D1M	64	64	C14	2	2
F1	68	68	D1X	1	1	C8	10	10
H	66	66	D3	34	34	D15	10	10
J	5	5	D3X	2	2	G16	4	4
L	37	37	E1	36	37	G6	34	34
N	65	65	E1R	10	10	H15	26	26
N1	6	1	E1X	1	1	H16	5	5
O	1	1	E2	10	10	K10	40	40
O1	55	55	E3	17	17	L&B 2-4-2T	1	1
P	8	8	E4	71	71	L&B 2-6-2T	4	4
Q1	0	2	E4X	4	4	L11	40	40
R	11	11	E5	26	26	L12	20	20
R1	13	13	E5X	4	4	Lord Nelson	16	16
RP	18	18	E6	10	10	M7	105	105
RP1	13	13	E6X	2	2	N15	74	74
S	1	1	H1	5	5	O2	44	46
T	10	10	H2	6	6	PDSWJ	3	3
U	40	40	I1	8	8	S11	10	10
U1	1	1	I1X	12	12	S15	35	35
Z	8	8	T14	10	10	T14	10	10
Total	644	649	I3	27	27	T14	50	50
			I4	5	5	T3	19	20
			J1	1	1	T6	10	10
			J2	1	1	T9	66	66
			K	17	17	V	10	0
			L	7	7	X3	19	20
			Total	520	538	X6	10	10
						Total	833	834

Table 3 Additional locomotives (321)

	Planned	Actual
Lord Nelson 4-6-0, increase from 16 to 46	30	0
L1 4-4-0, increase from 37 to 68	31	0
N and N1, increase from 72 to 77 (N 76 to 91) (N1 to 16)	5	15
S15 4-6-0, increase from 35 to 53	18	0
U and U1 2-6-0, increase from 41 to 106 (U 40 to 50) (U1 1 to 21)	65	30
V Schools 4-4-0, increase from 10 to 76	66	30
W (noted as 4-6-2 goods tanks), 25 new (all on Central Division)	25	15
Y 0-6-0 freight shunter 69, but revised so 9 of 51 Eastern Division duties to be Z 0-8-0T	60	0
Z 0-8-0 freight tank, increase from 8 to 20, i.e. 11 plus 9 from Y Class	20	0

Table 4 Locomotives to be scrapped from 1.1.1931 figure (244)

LSWR A12 0-4-2, reduced from 68 to 25	43
LSWR X2, T3, T6, X6, C8 4-4-0, reduced by 68	68
LSWR 0330 0-6-0ST, reduction of 5	5
LBSC B1 Gladstone 0-4-2, reduction of 3	3
LBSC B2X 4-4-0, reduction of 9	9
LBSC E1 0-6-0T, reduction of 36	36
LBSC I tanks, reduction of 5	5
SER B1 4-4-0, reduction of 27	27
LCDR B2 0-6-0, reduction of 4	4
LCDR T 0-6-0T, reduction of 10	10
SER R and R1 0-6-0T, reduction of 24	24
Total of goods 0-6-0s reduced from 259 to 249*	10

* This entry covers LSWR 700 Class (30), Brighton C2, C2X and C3 Classes (65) and SECR O, O1 (56) and C (108) Classes. The Central Division total to be reduced from 65 to 45, with about 8 locos going to the Western Division and 2 to the Eastern Division, presumably replacing older locomotives to be withdrawn.

Building and scrapping programme

The Traffic Department wanted a lot more express locomotives; assuming that the extra 'L1s' would continue to provide the Kent Coast services, it is hard to see how thirty extra 'Lord Nelsons' and sixty-six 'Schools' would have been employed elsewhere. Perhaps O. V. S. Bulleid saw these figures when justifying the construction of his 'Pacifics'. Certainly the total of engines to be scrapped, at 244, is less than the 321 additional locomotives. As we know, the economic situation meant that the Board refused to authorise new construction unless an equivalent number of older engines were replaced.

The modest increase in N class engines is overshadowed by the proposal for an extra sixty 'U' Class engines. These 2-6-0s were in fact augmented by the reconstruction of the twenty 'River' Class 2-6-4 tanks.

The proposal for the 'Y' Class 0-6-0 had been in place since 1927, according to D. L. Bradley, but would be overtaken by the economy and the adoption of diesel engine shunters in the mid-1930s.

Availability

Some conclusions on availability assumptions can be drawn from the above categories. Tables 5 and 6 summarise the situation by Division and by extracting the data for the designs originated or perpetuated by the Southern Railway: overall 73% (66% Cat A plus 7% Cat B) of the locomotive stock was assumed to be available for traffic, whereas the more modern designs achieved an availability of 84% – these figures would have been used by Maunsell to justify further new construction. Similarly, nearly 16% of locomotives were out of service for repair (C plus D) compared to less than 10% of modern designs.

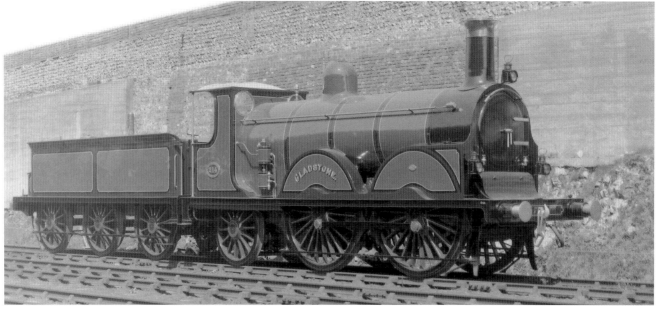

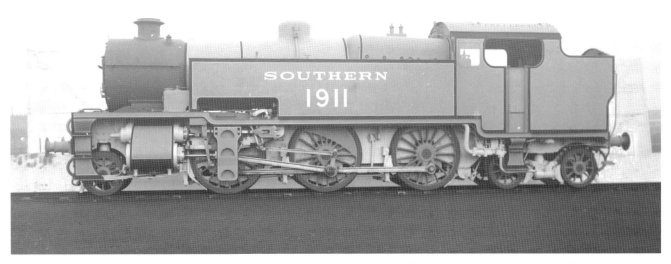

The unmistakable outline of a 'W' Class 2-6-4T, fifteen of which were built between 1930 and 1936 out of a proposed twenty-five. Had the Southern not had such an aversion to using large tank engines on passenger services, numbers may even have been increased further. Of interest here is the background to this 'works grey' view taken at Eastleigh: note how the photographer has had a wooden screen placed behind the engine to block out unnecessary detail.

This is clearly Eastleigh Works, but in LSWR days (an Adams 4-4-0 and two Drummond engines are visible). No doubt Eastleigh would have played a major part in the construction of the proposed additional engines, although, as can be seen from Table 3, out of the planned 320, only ninety were actually built.

Opposite top: 'A12' No 616 was one class whose numbers were to be reduced, although the type as a whole was not planned to be culled. Instead, numbers would be reduced from sixty-eight to twenty-five: No 616 succumbed in 1936. In fact, sixty-eight of the type were indeed withdrawn in the years 1931 through to 1948. Two of those supposed still 'active' in the period 1939-45, Nos 625 and 638, were used as 'air-raid shelters' at Eastleigh, where they were placed over a pit and surrounded by a wall of sandbags. (No 625 had been officially withdrawn in January 1939 but was reinstated in October 1939 and survived in capital stock until 1947.)

Middle: As with the LSWR 'A12' design, so the LBSCR equivalent, the 'B' Class, was to be culled, but this time totally. No 214, seen here, had been preserved in 1927. Again, on paper at least, two engines survived beyond 1931. Their demise would be swift, with the final example, No 172 *Littlehampton*, withdrawn in 1933.

Bottom: Had the proposed new builds taken place, there would have been an additional twenty members of the 'Z' Class, intended for heavy shunting where loads were increasing. As is known, the advent of the more versatile diesel shunter would negate the need for further examples of the type, although they continued to prove their worth on both shunting and banking duties.

Table 5 Summary of availability (all designs)

Division	A	B	C	D	E	Total
Western	540	67	67	56	90	820
Central	320	27	51	45	72	515
Eastern	442	52	40	54	46	634
	1,302	146	158	155	208	1,969
	66.1%	7.4%	8.0%	7.9%	10.6%	

A = Booked duties B = Special duties C = Engines under repair at depot D = Engines in or awaiting shops E = Spare at depots

Table 6 Availability for SR-built locomotives

Division	A	B	C	D	E	Total
SR designs	387	63	21	31	35	537
	72.1%	11.7%	3.9%	5.8%	6.5%	

A = Booked duties B = Special duties C = Engines under repair at depot D = Engines in or awaiting shops E = Spare at depots

The SLS *Journal* of 1931, page 57, reported the Southern 1931 building programme as:

15 2-6-0 goods tender engines

10 0-8-0T shunting engines

5 2-6-4T goods engines

In fact, no more 'Z' Class tanks were constructed, but more 'U' and 'N' 2-6-0 engines were built than planned.

Conclusion

This document gives an insight into how the Traffic Department saw its need for locomotives. The whole picture is different as the Civil Engineer, Mechanical Engineer and Board had their perceptions. It is probably always true that the Traffic Department will take an optimistic view of the maintenance or growth of traffic. Thus this document represents the 'high' bid, which would be reduced by engineering constraints and the reality of the capital and revenue accounts.

Table 7 Western Division

Class	Nine Elms	Feltham	Guildford	Basingstoke	Eastleigh	Fratton LSWR	Bournemouth	Dorchester	Salisbury	Yeovil	Exmouth Jct	Barnstaple	Wadebridge	Plymouth Friary	Total
LN 4-6-0 Lord Nelson	14				7		9								30
LSWR A12 0-4-2			10		7	2			6						25
LSWR B4 0-4-0T					19		2							4	25
LSWR 700 LBSCR C2X 0-6-0	2	12	6		11		1	2			4				38
LBSC D1, D1M, D1X (Lyme Regis) 0-4-2T			2		2	3				2	4			2	15
LSWR D15 4-4-0						10									10
LSWR G6 0-6-0T	8	1	8				1	1	5	2	8				34
LSWR G16 4-8-0T & H16 4-6-2T		9													9
LSWR H15 4-6-0	19				3				4						26
LSWR K10 4-4-0	3	2	1	3	11	3		1	4	4	2				34
LSWR L12 4-4-0	1		3		7	3	6								20
LSWR L11 4-4-0	5	4	1		11	9	7		1	1	1				40
LSWR M7 0-4-4T	28	17	21		7	1	15				7	6			102
N15 4-6-0	26				2		1		11		10				50
N & N1 2-6-0									5	3	33	6			47
LSWR O2 0-4-4T	6			3	2			7		1	17		3	5	44
LSWR 0395 0-6-0		7	5	1	4						3				20
LSWR & SR S15 4-6-0	6	18			1				5		6				36
LSWR S11 4-4-0						6					4				10
LSWR T14 4-6-0	10														10
LSWR T9 4-4-0					10	2		9	20	8	8			9	66
LSWR T1 0-4-4T	4	3		1	3	2	7		3		3			4	30
U & U1 2-6-0	9		25	11		10									55
Y 0-6-0 freight shunter				1	12										13
Z 0-8-0T freight shunter					1				1		1				3
LSWR 0458 0-4-0T			1		1										2
LBSC E1R 0-6-2T												10			10
LSWR 0298 2-4-0T													3		3
Lynton & Barnstaple												5			5
PDSWJR 756 0-6-0T															
757 & 758 0-6-2T					1									2	3
LSWR 0415 4-4-2T											2				2
LSWR C14 0-4-0T					3										3
Total	141	73	83	20	125	51	49	20	65	21	113	27	6	26	820

Table 8 Central Division

Class	Battersea Park	New Cross Gate	West Croydon	Tunbridge Wells	West Horsham	Three Little Bridges	Hampton	Bognor	Brighton	Newhaven	Eastbourne	St Leonards	Fratton LBSC	Total
LBSC A1 0-6-0T							1		2	2			4	9
LBSC B4X 4-4-0	5	4							3					12
LBSC B4 4-4-0		7							12				2	21
LBSCR C2 & C2X 0-6-0	5	5		10				2	11	5	3		4	45
SECR C 0-6-0												3		3
SECR D & E 4-4-0												7		7
SECR D1 & E1 4-4-0												2		2
LBSC D1, D1M 0-4-2T	2			3	10		6	7	22	4	6			60
LBSC D3 & D3X 0-4-4T				12							8	7		27
LBSC E2-E6X 0-6-2T	19	44	12		6	21		4	23	2	7		7	145
LBSCR H1 & H2 4-4-2									4	2	5			11
LBSCR I1X & I4 4-4-2T				5				1	3	1	3			13
LBSCR I1, I2 & I3 4-4-2T	8	5		4	7			1	16	2	1			44
LBSCR J 4-6-2T	2													2
LBSCR K 2-6-0	2	5							4	1	3		2	17
LBSC L 4-6-4T								7						7
SECR L & L1 4-4-0									3			2		5
S15 4-6-0	4	2							1					7
U & U1 2-6-0	9	4												13
V 4-4-0 Schools	7	3							4	1	10	12		37
W 2-6-4T	13	11				1								25
Y 0-6-0 freight shunter												2		2
Z 0-8-0T freight shunter		1												1
Total	76	91	12	24	33	22	7	22	108	20	46	35	19	515

Table 9 Eastern Division

Class	Battersea	Bricklayers Arms	Gillingham	Maidstone East	Maidstone West	Faversham	Redhill	Reading	Tonbridge	Ashford	Canterbury West	Ramsgate	Folkestone	Dover	Total
LN 4-6-0 Lord Nelson	16														16
SECR C or 'New' SR C 0-6-0	28	50	13		5	9	10		24	9	2	7	6	2	163
SECR D1 & E1 4-4-0		2	6				11		3	8					30
LBSC D3 & D3X 0-4-4T									5						5
SECR D & E 4-4-0		7	13	9	4							5			38
SECR H 0-4-4T	16	14	6		1					2	2	13		12	66
SECR J 0-6-4T		5													5
SECR L & L1 4-4-0	12	13				9			14	6				9	63
LSWR K10 4-4-0								6							6
LSWR M7 0-4-4T								3							3
N15 4-6-0	9											10		5	24
N & N1 2-6-0	4	10				3	7	1	3					2	30
SECR P 0-6-0T										1			1	6	8
R & R1 0-4-4T	2		4		2	5		4	1	2		1	10		31
S15 4-6-0	4	6													10
U & U1 2-6-0	26							10	1	1					38
V 4-4-0 Schools		17							3	2		13		4	39
Y 0-6-0 freight shunter	8	15	4		2	2	4	4	2	5	1	1		6	54
Z 0-8-0T freight shunter		3	1							1					5
Total	125	142	47	9	14	28	32	28	53	40	5	50	17	44	634

Table 10 Actual allocation of engines to Central Division, 4 April 1929

Class	Battersea Park	New Cross Gate	West Croydon	Tunbridge Wells W	Horsham	Three Bridges	Littlehampton	Bognor	Brighton Works	Brighton	Newhaven	Eastbourne	St Leonards	Fratton LBSC	Eastern Section	Western Section	Stored	Total
A1									1									1
A1X							1			5	1			3				10
B1	1					1				7			2					11
B2X	3	8											5	6				22
B4	4	4						2		9		2						21
B4X	4	4								4								12
C2	2	3				2				2	3	2						14
C2X	8	11			2	2		2		6	3	2	2	3				41
C3		4			6													10
D1		2								3			1			4		10
D1M			4	4	12		8	5		10	2	8		3			8	64
D1X								1										1
D3				12						5		9	6					34
D3X										2								2
E1		9	3		3	4		1		9	5	5		2	1			37
E1R																10		10
E1X					1													1
E2	4	6																10
E3		5	5					1			3	3			3			17
E4	9	18	8	1		11				14		6		4				71
E4X		4																4
E5	6	9			3	6						2						26
E5X		2			2													4
E6	10																	10
E6X	2																	2
H1										3	2							5
H2								4		1	1							6
I1							2	1		7								10
I1X	3	2			5													10
I2										10								10
I3	15	6								6								27
I4				5														5
J1										1								1
J2										1								1
K	3	7								5				2				17
L										7								7
L12														7				7
N15										14								14
U												10						10
Total	76	99	20	22	33	26	11	17	1	133	20	45	16	30	4	14	8	575

Southern Region colour
Part 1 Mainly east of Southampton

Roger Holmes

An introduction to the colour slide collection of Roger Holmes has already been given in this issue's Editorial, so it may be convenient to launch straight in with a little detail followed by the appropriate descriptions. According to his notebooks, Roger would use a variety of colour film, Kodachrome 1, Kodachrome 2, Ectachrome, and AgfaColour. The slow speed of many of these films did mean images of moving trains were on occasions variable, while just as noticeable is the variation in colour associated with each. Of course a sunny day helped considerably and when it worked, it certainly worked well.

'East of Southampton' is a term that perhaps requires slight explanation in that we are referring to the railway east of Southampton 'turning right' at St Denys to take the 'Southampton & Netley' route towards Fareham. This view is on the outskirts of St Denys and shows 'T9' No 30707 heading north and just about to pass under Priory Road footbridge. St Denys signal box may also be seen. Roger rarely recorded the actual working and to be fair his notes are perhaps literally just that – 'a note'. Accordingly he states that this is simply a 'van train', and does not even give the loco number (which we can determine for ourselves). The leading vehicle is a GWR 'Syphon G', but these vehicles could well stray from their former haunts, so while it is tempting to suggest that this is a service bound for the Western Region it cannot be confirmed. The view was taken in November 1960 in what would be the engine's last few months of service as withdrawal came in March 1961. In the left background is the unmistakable outline of the cab and bunker of a BR 4MT 2-6-4T, which we will see in more detail in the next picture.

The south end of St Denys was also the northern exit from Bevois Park goods yard, where close to the appropriately named Drummond Road were two sidings especially provided for locomotive purposes. The vantage point is Horseshoe Bridge, from which we see the aforementioned 'Standard 4' No 80011 and an unidentified diesel shunter. (Roger was without doubt a steam man for while he would record some steam loco numbers, that was rarely the case with other forms of traction.) As in so many views from the period, it is not just the main subject that is of interest – notice the telegraph pole, the concrete bin used by the permanent way gang for small chippings – a product of the concrete works at Exmouth Junction, of course – and the white surround to the red lamp on the buffer stop. Away from the railway, washing is hanging on a line – this might come in dry but I suspect also covered in smuts. No 80011 looks relatively fresh from overhaul and also displays electrification warning 'flashes'. (See *SW23* for an article on Bevois Park sidings.)

Roger's third view at this location taken on the same occasion shows No 34098 *Templecombe* on a through working to Cardiff via Southampton Central, hence the headcode. (A Southern Region Mk 1 set still in crimson and cream forms the front of the train.) The engine is now accelerating, having slowed for the sharp curve both on the approach to and the exit from the Netley line platforms at St Denys. Three months later the engine would be taken into Eastleigh Works for rebuilding. Notice on the extreme left the water column on the engine sidings referred to previously. The gradient post in its faded green paint and the railway allotments are also now but memories.

This picture shows the sharp curve at the approach to St Denys from the east. The engine is one not so often seen in colour, No 34033 *Chard*, with front fairing removed and cut-down tender but still retaining a square cab. The train is an inter-regional working from Portsmouth to the Western Region, recorded in January 1961, again with a numbered Southern Region Mk 1 set at the head, but this time painted in green.

Eastleigh was clearly determined to get as much use out of No 30707 while it could (was she eventually withdrawn due a management directive or because of a defect had been discovered that did not warrant repair?). Whatever, she is seen here earning here keep on the climb towards Woolston and with the River Itchen in the background. The passenger working is probably covering for a failed diesel set, and has been strengthened with the addition of two vans at the rear. At this point the train is on a rising gradient of 1 in 90, hence the catch points to protect against runaways.

The more usual stopping service on the Netley line at the time was a three-car DEMU set, this example being No 1126. The number '43' in the headcode signified a Portsmouth working, while the yellow 'V' was a dual-purpose innovation. True, it assisted in warning anyone on the track of the pending approach of the train, but it should be noted that there was no corresponding 'V' at the opposite end. (Some sets had the 'V' in a much darker, orange shade.) Primarily the 'V' was to assist station staff in identifying which end of the set had the luggage compartment so that they could start to push any barrows along the platform so as to be at the correct end – not always easy on a congested platform. The sets might work with either end leading, so this was a necessary feature compared with the steam trains they had replaced, which invariably had a brake compartment and therefore luggage space at either end. Unit No 1126 (later No 205026) was scrapped in 1990.

This time it is set No 1124 – luggage compartment at the opposite end – that is recorded at the same spot. Notice the orange-painted handrails, which corresponded exactly to the colour of the 'V' on some sets. No 1124 became No 205024 and after a life of 41 years was scrapped in 2000.

This final view of the approach to Woolston in November 1960 has our familiar 'T9' No 30707 again, but this time with a simple two-coach parcels working. The introduction of the 'Hampshire' diesel multiple unit scheme on branch and cross-country workings quickly brought about difficulties in accommodating luggage and parcels on some lines, and in consequence it was not unknown for a steam-hauled parcels service to operate over the same route as the diesel at least once daily. (More on this topic can be found in the articles by Richard Simmons describing 'Southampton Control' that appeared in *SW* issues 6, 8, 12 and 16.)

Right: **Certain engines were regular performers on specific routes at this time, as witness No 34098 *Templecombe* again descending the bank past Woolston with an inter-regional working from Brighton.**

Below: **This time it is the turn of rebuilt 'West Country' No 34014 *Budleigh Salterton* to have charge of a similar working; the use of WR coaching stock will be noted.**

Moving east to Woolston station itself, in October 1959 Roger recorded this rather grimy unidentified two-car DEMU set arriving on a stopping service to Portsmouth. The replacement of steam trains by these diesel sets was not without difficulty; a diesel set formation initially of just two vehicles meant that there was insufficient passenger accommodation, and they were also regarded as excessively noisy. Both issues were addressed, the former simply by the addition of a third coach. Perhaps surprisingly there does not appear to be any indication of a set number above the headcode. Notice also that, despite the motor coach and therefore luggage compartment leading, no 'V' indication has yet been added. The ground disc signal at bottom right referred to a trailing crossover the extreme far end of which can just be discerned behind the second coach.

The main station building at Woolston dates back to the 1880s and was similar in style to the buildings at St Denys and Netley (at the latter the building is listed Grade 2). Photographed by Roger in October 1959, the goods shed and station footbridge are also in view while in the background are various recently built tower blocks on what is the Weston housing estate.

On 13 April 1960 No 76059 was recorded at Netley leaving the up running line and about to enter the goods yard – possibly this was to enable a loaded van to be nearer the station entrance. The engine is certainly less than clean and still retains its original as-built crest on the tender. The train is at present 'wrong road', a situation that will be explained further in the next view. Trains on the St Denys to Fareham line worked 'up' towards Southampton and 'down' towards Fareham.

'Standard 4' No 75065 is also 'wrong road' at Netley. Roger recorded several instances of non-passenger trains in this situation, which begs the obvious question, 'why'? One answer could simply be that the train has been shunted to allow a following service to pass. However, another clue may come from the formation of this particular service: the engine may be about to pull into the yard and push/collect vehicles from one of the sidings accessible in this way, or the engine could be about to run round and perform likewise in a different siding. (There were crossovers between the running lines at both ends of the station.) With some thought the last-named move may be the most likely, not least because Roger recorded a train in this type of position several times, but it was always complete, never with a full run-round or shunt move shown. The conclusion is therefore perhaps that the vans at the rear of the train were to be accessed and it was certainly a lot easier to load goods to and from the down platform where there was direct access to the station approach.

In July 1960 our old friend No 30707 is 'wrong road' at Netley with a parcels train. There was no road access to the opposite platform, so as mentioned above it is likely that this was a regular move with this type of service.

After being superseded from their original haunts on the Eastern section, a few former SECR 4-4-0s found their way to Nine Elms, Basingstoke and Eastleigh for further use. 'D1' No 31725 was one of these, being recorded at Netley on parcels in February or March 1961. (Note this time that the engine is running on the correct line towards Fareham.) Officially withdrawn at the end of August 1960, the engine was clearly reinstated for a time but would finally meet its end in September 1961.

This superb portrayal of a Class 4MT 2-6-4T shows it engaged in shunting at Netley some time in the spring of 1961; what is possibly a vehicle buffer from the remainder of the train may just be glimpsed on the extreme right. Were the children just watching the scene or was there something else happening?

An early casualty among the Bulleid breed was No 34055 *Fighter Pilot*, seen here awaiting departure from Netley but clearly with steam to spare. As photographed here in the early summer of 1961, the engine retains its original BR crest and has the original high raves to the tender, and black lining. Clearly it was a reliable machine for it is recorded as running just under 70,000 miles between February 1960 and September 1961. Unfortunately, in April 1963 it was in charge of a similar Brighton to Cardiff through working when it failed at Chichester with what was subsequently diagnosed as a cracked middle cylinder. Three other original engines, Nos, 34035, 34043 and 34074, were already laid up at Exmouth Junction with various defects pending a decision as to their future, and that decision was that all four would be withdrawn. Had the option been taken to perhaps salvage parts from one of these engines, perhaps the others would have had a reprieve, but that was not to be and, together with its three sisters, No 34055 had the dubious distinction of being among the first Bulleid 'Pacifics' to be withdrawn. None of the four would escape the scrap merchant.

West of Netley and trailing into the up line was the private siding for British Petroleum, as described earlier in this issue. Roger did not record the engine number seen here in the spring of 1961, although from the first coach we may be certain it is either a through or special working.

An unidentified member of the 'N' Class on a passenger duty passes through Netley cutting. Clearly this was a warm spring day as witness the predominance of open droplights.

On a crisp, bright January morning in 1961 No 34038 *Lynton* is seen entering Bursledon from the direction of Swanwick on yet another inter-regional service. This time the point of interest must be the different coloured rakes of rolling stock, all of the BR Mk 1 type but in the contrasting liveries of the period. At this time the engine was based at Brighton, but was transferred to Eastleigh in the autumn of 1961.

This time we have one of the rebuilt Bulleid types clearly passing through Bursledon bound for Southampton and beyond. Other than 'November 1960', Roger recorded no other details. Two things are of particular interest here. First, the rolling stock – could it be a train of maroon coaches, and if so was that unusual for such a service? Note also the goods yard sidings, which had been officially closed just a few weeks earlier on 12 September but were not formally taken out of use until September 1961. Even so, it appears some time since a vehicle of any sort ran on the rails – with the exception of the four-wheel platelayers' trolley by the shadow of the bridge, complete with shovel!

In our final view on the Netley line, Roger has the engine recorded as No 34006, but that cannot be correct; it is in fact No 34008 *Padstow*, seen in January 1961 just seven months after having been rebuilt. The low angle of the view, again near Bursledon, accentuates the dramatic appearance of the rebuilt members of the class – although that is of course a subjective opinion. One spotter from the 1950s recounted his first sighting of a rebuilt Bulleid compared with the originals and recalled, 'At first I thought it was a "Britannia" that was approaching…'

For the final two images in this selection (and to give a hint about future views to come) we move away from the immediate environs of the Netley line and instead travel east to Portsmouth & Southsea where in June 1960 'Schools' No 30904 *Lancing* was recorded in, shall we say, 'travel-worn' condition. This would also be last full year of service for No 30904 – as it would be also for most of her sister members of the class. It is by now based at Basingstoke, which would also be its final depot.

Looking through Roger's records, he appears to have taken an average of one roll of colour film per month; October 1960 saw eighteen recorded images on Agfacolour, although only four were railway-related. One of these is seen here, taken from a down train passing Basingstoke shed with two engines, a Standard Class 5, possibly No 73042, and an unidentified 'Schools'. The contrast in the workaday grime of the steam engines against the freshly painted open wagon behind is remarkable – the latter would certainly not stay pristine for long.

Seeing life in black and white

'Photographic grey' was used by the LSWR, LBSCR and SECR, and as here with certain items highlighted in white. This is ostensibly No 850 *Lord Nelson* in original condition – or so we are meant to believe!

Readers might be forgiven for expecting what follows to be a hypothesis on the merits (or otherwise) of seeing our railway history in black and white. Indeed, we are well used to viewing life 50 or more years ago in this medium rather than in colour, and certainly the further back in time one looks the greater the percentage of two-dimensional and, if we can use the phrase in general terms, 'two-dimensional colour', there is available.

All the railway companies recorded their new products in this way. For the sake of keeping a record of a new locomotive, structure or occasion, black and white photography was the best (indeed almost the only) option available, while in the case of locomotives – new, rebuilt, or perhaps modified in some form – 'photographic grey' was used, the engine deliberately painted this way with certain parts sometimes highlighted in white paint. Experience had shown that rather than use the actual company colours, which were often dark, grey was found to give the best contrast results when the image was seen in printed form. Later on, and back in the photographer's studio, the background would on occasions be painted out. This removal of irrelevant detail was intended to reduce distractions and so highlight the actual subject matter. Certainly it achieved its purpose, but from the perspective of historians and researchers today it is often a delight to study various items of rolling stock, locomotives or other detail that are seen in these backgrounds and which might otherwise

have been lost.

Where are we going with this theme? Well, something happened in the summer of 2015 which, with hindsight, might well be regarded as obvious but as far as I am aware has never been studied in detail previously.

We need first to go back to the autumn of 2014 and a visit made to the National Railway Museum by several member of the South Western Circle to view the collection of negatives recently acquired for the nation by the NRM from the estate of the late Barry Curl. Many of these are of London & South Western Railway origin and out of the scope of the present text.

I was privileged to be part of this team, although for personal reasons I was unable to spend the complete week at York with other circle members, as had been intended; even so, I spent two very enjoyable days viewing, scanning and discussing the items, many of which had probably not been seen for decades.

Our purpose at York was to scan as many of these negatives as possible (a few having since appeared in *SW* as well as in the 'Circle' magazine). Included in the collection were items other than negatives, principally rolls of locomotive drawings, which I did not view on the days spent at York, and also one book, a register, which now forms the basis for the topic under discussion.

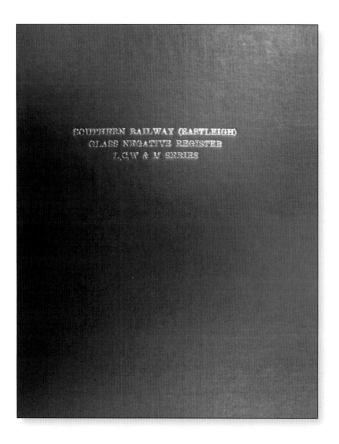

This register is one I don't think any of us knew existed and provides in handwritten form a record of the complete 'Southern Railway (Eastleigh). Glass Negative Register. L, C, W & M Series'. (It was quickly established that the initials must refer Locomotives (350 entries), Carriages (circa 350 entries), Wagons (105 entries) and Miscellaneous (slightly in excess of 865 entries). Dates are not always given, while against the reference 'size' it is usually 12 x 10 or half-plate that is recorded, but again with gaps. The register itself appears to cover the years from soon after the Grouping into the first years of BR, and includes some copy negatives.

While such registers would certainly have existed and been used up to the mid-1960s, after that time it became policy to discard much of what was then perceived as obsolete, hence it was a wonderful feeling to establish that such an important record had survived.

Important, most certainly. But why? Well, simply because scrawled across its pages are references to negatives taken to record actual prototype items we may not always have known existed, absolute manna for the researcher. This is in addition to information on additional images or topics where perhaps just a single view was all that had ever been seen before. This additional information could also throw up questions that were not known to exist beforehand.

As an example in the latter category is negative reference No L102. No date is given, but in the other columns across the page (the negative number is in the first column) we have Engine No E850, then the size of the negative (in this case 12 x 10) followed by a column headed 'View', in this case stated to be a '3/4 view'. Finally there is an unheaded column where any remarks or additional notes were made, and it is in this column that we find a rather interesting annotation: 'Lord Nelson, E861 painted as No 850'. In fact, negatives L102, 103 and 104 all continue the deceit, showing No E861 not just from the front but also on all sides and in each case masquerading as No 850. We do of course know that engines might swap identities from time to time, with particularly well-known examples having existed on the GWR and LMS, but I had honestly thought the Southern was above such treachery; however, here it was in black and white!

A little later in the series comes a long sequence from L125 through to L201, this time nearly all depicting 'Schools' Class engines from No 910 *Merchant Taylors* to No 939 *Leatherhead*. All have the same basic two poses, broadside and a three-quarter front view, including Nos L159/160 of No 923 *Uppingham* and with an appended note 'now Bradfield see L211/212'. There are just eight exceptions in this long list where other engines feature. In the light of the above can we now be certain that all these 'Schools' Class engines were actually different machines or were a select few simply renumbered and renamed for the occasion? Unfortunately dates are not given.

Even so, with a bit of detective work it may be possible now to start identifying possible dates and information with reference to some of the more common 'official'-type images of various Southern types, hopefully adding data to our existing knowledge.

No 850 is seen again, but this time later and with the addition of smoke-deflectors. Most official views at Eastleigh were taken outside the front of the Works and with, as here, the background later painted out. This particular view might well have been a winter image, which clearly shows the disadvantage of a low angle of the sun accentuated by the standard livery. We may assume that it was also a reject so far as the photographic studio was concerned, as the shadow of the photographer, his assistant and camera remain, all of which would otherwise have been removed.

Here is a better attempt with a different angle, probably on the same occasion and, from the ground shadow, slightly later in the day.

So far as missing views are concerned, most *SW* readers will be familiar with the two well-known images of the solitary 'Schools' No 999 (temporarily renamed from No 935 *Sevenoaks*) bedecked with plywood streamlining and seen either head-on or as a left broadside view. But it transpires that these are in fact just two of eight views of the same experiment, four of which are broadside, with three-quarter images and the head-on view already known of. These are referred to as 'Version A'. There then follows 'Version B', again a series of four images from varying angles. As we know, just the two commonly seen images of No 999 have been published, so what happened to the other six, and do versions 'A' and 'B' refer to different attempts at photographing the engine in its streamlined guise, or are we even looking at a reference to two versions of the streamlining? Whatever the answer, it is certainly new information on all counts. The actual negatives examined included a number that appear to be from this register, but unfortunately the missing ones in this series are not present.

Generally, some of the references also have an addendum such as 'to H.O.' ('to Head Office'), or 'to Mr so and so B'ton', occasionally with a date but sometimes not. So far as the negatives obtained from Mr Curl are concerned, a trawl through all of them (several hundred) does not find these extra views. Are they then somewhere in the bowels of the NRM, were they loaned officially, or even broken accidentally or on purpose?

The Carriage and Wagon listings (there are fewer entries on wagons) reveal nothing that perhaps immediately stands out, although there is an intriguing short series on camping coaches, with both exterior and interior views. Do they survive?

The Miscellaneous category is by far the largest section and includes subjects as diverse as workshop equipment; incidents (signal wire around axle of wagon); Hudd's train control; locomotive components (most of the 'L' series are complete engines); workshop accidents; and component failures. An example is the sequence M829 through to M835, with views of a broken crank pin on No 35024. This includes the actual driving wheel and bends on the associated coupling rod. The

date of the incident is not reported in the register, although the sequence was taken commencing on 29 September 1950. There does not appear to be any mention in the usual sources relating to this occurrence, despite checking the *Railway Observer*, D. L. Bradley's volumes on *Locomotives of the Southern Railway*, and the *Book of the Merchant Navy class*. (For reference only and to indicate the variety with this 'M' sequence, the preceding image, No M828, is an accident to a workman on the finishing shop circular saw, and No M836 is of the Eastleigh Fire Brigade.)

Regardless of the series, nearly all the entries are views taken at Eastleigh itself, one of the few exceptions being on 8 March 1945 when Nos M689/1 and M689/2 show the 'Salisbury Engine Hoist, Fixed Hoist with engine No 2157 in both up and down positions'.

Readers will be familiar with the author's continuing interest in the 'Leader' Class, which is represented in the collection in part form with six views of the complete boiler and firebox, recorded on either 25 August, 3 September or 7 September 1948. (Were these all of the same boiler or different boilers completed shortly after each other?) Further component images are referred to on 7 July 1950: 'flawed crank axle' has four images, although the entries for each have been crossed through. This is immediately followed by a further four views again referring to a broken crank axle on the 'Leader'. (We know that there was such a failure while on trial from Eastleigh. Again, none of these negatives appear to have survived and your author is 99% certain they were never at the NRM.)

The only other entries for No 36001 are on 25 May 1951 at the time it was being broken up, and again show the boiler and firebox assembly from four different angles – but again only one view is actually known.

No 999 (really No 935 *Sevenoaks*) has been temporarily made up with wooden streamlining. Some commentators have suggested that the engine actually worked a test train in this condition as far as Micheldever, but the jury must still be out on that story. The other known view is almost head-on but, as recounted in the text, what of the other images in both this and the other similarly listed series? Were there in fact two versions of this streamlining?

Why this is in turn significant is that we know that a series of official images were taken of No 36001 during its first visit to Eastleigh as a completed engine in July 1950. This was the occasion when it was recorded from both the ends and sides and with the engine number shown centrally under the BR crest midway along the casing. None of these official views appear in the register presently under discussion, so clearly there was at least one other official register, and this is confirmed via the NRM website when it speaks of an 'Eastleigh Works' photographic list. (So far as the Southern and its constituents are concerned, there are also specific 'Ashford Works', 'Brighton Locomotive Works', and 'LBSCR' lists, while there is at least one other NRM list. In addition, the NRM make reference to a 'Clapham [BTC]' list, which may hold Southern material.)

What all this tells us, whether reader or enthusiast, historian or researcher, is that despite the main facts and figures on our locomotives and rolling stock – indeed, our whole railway history – being well-known and documented, there are still any number of additional pieces to fit into the knowledge jigsaw. Perhaps the incident involving No 35024 in 1950 is the typical example. The actual locomotive may have been withdrawn and cut up for recycling into razor blades or whatever more than 50 years ago, yet here is a new piece of information to add to its history. It also goes to elucidate why, in the Derry/Sixsmith 'Book of...' volume, the works records for No 35024 show 'LC' (Light Casual) from 11 July 1950 to 18 August 1950 with a reported mileage of 86,621, then a further 'LC' works visit with exactly the same mileage from 13 September to 6 October 1950. We may conclude that No 35024 had indeed been repaired, then suffered the aforementioned failure probably on a trial trip, the mileage for which was not recorded. The engine was thus returned to works around 13 September (official dates for arrival/departure may well be slightly inaccurate) and lay around for a little while until photographed. Having been recorded, the necessary repair was completed rapidly and No 35024 returned to its home depot at Exmouth Junction soon afterwards.

This is one of a series of photographs depicting the boiler and firebox from No 36001 during dismantling of the engine in 1951. The distortion caused to the firebox side sheeting – albeit relatively thin sheet – is immediately apparent. Ostensibly one of several taken at the time, the question is perhaps 'why record the scene'? The 'Leader' project was now condemned and would not be resurrected, so was this simply a series of images inside the works?

Terry Cole's Rolling Stock Files

No 31 Isle of Wight goods stock (2)

This is DS426, an ex-Isle of Wight Railway 10-ton travelling crane built in 1876 by James Taylor of Birkenhead. It is seen here in the summer of 1965 together with its match truck DS3138 stored out of the way in the up siding at Brading. Some fresh paint has been applied and it looks to be in good order. The odd locomotive, awaiting works or simply not needed for traffic, was often also stored here even in the summer months.

Photographs by Terry Cole

If the Isle of Wight traffic stock was ancient, then the Engineers and Service Department stock was positively antique. Many vehicles found a home in some little-used siding where they stayed for months (perhaps years) on end.

The business part of the Island's weed-killing train was formed of two ex-Isle of Wight Central Railway tar/water tanks, Nos 140/141. Nearest the camera is SR 443s (the former IWCR No 140) with SR 428s in black beyond. Presumably they made a tour of the Island's lines each spring, but they look very much 'out to grass' here on the spur of the old Newport line at Sandown in the summer of 1965.

Here at last is a service vehicle not stuck in a siding. No DS439 started life as Isle of Wight Railway carriage truck No 76. The Southern renumbered it 4380, then in 1930 converted it to a boiler trolley and gave it the number 439s. The wagon has a saddle at one end to support the bottom of the boiler/smokebox barrel and a large hole in the floor the other end to take the firebox. Renumbered again by BR as DS439, it is seen here in the summer of 1965 outside Ryde St John's Works.

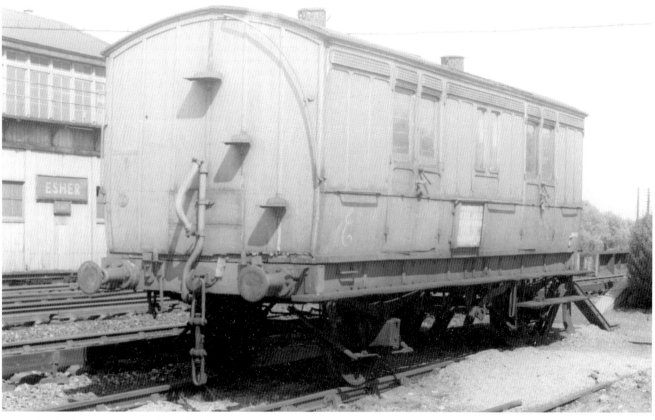

No 32 Four ancient non-passenger vehicles

Photographs by David Wigley

This antique vehicle, No S064, is an ex-London & South Western Railway 24-foot Luggage Van of 1897, and is seen here at Esher (east) on 3 May 1959. Note the arc roof (predating the typical elliptical shape) and the two 'lamp pots'.

In the 1950s and even in the early 1960s there were still a number of old vehicles hiding away in sidings in 'Departmental' use.

Here is another ex-LSWR van, this time with the later style of roof. It is No 919S, which in 1904 had a new body built on the underframe of an earlier 18-foot Luggage Van.

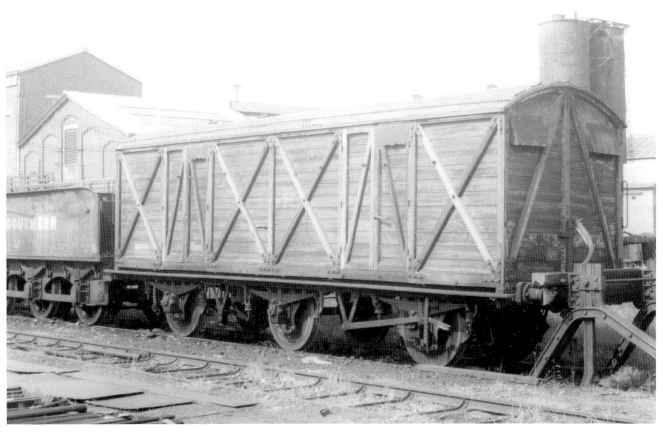

The South Eastern Railway in particular liked separate vehicles for the guard and luggage on its passenger trains. The SER/SECR had two main six-wheeled designs of Passenger Brake Van, both about 32 feet long. The type with the centre 'birdcage' roof and side lookouts we have seen in Rolling Stock File No 12. This is the other type with side 'duckets' at each end, and is pictured at Exeter Central close to the end of its days.

No 1648s is an unusual-looking six-wheeled van with outside framing. It was built by the London, Brighton & South Coast Railway and is seen here tucked away in a siding at the back of Eastleigh Works on 7 August 1957.

Stewarts Lane steam shed

Above: As is probably well known, the Offices, Shops and Railway Premises Act of 1963 was intended to ensure that workers had a safe, comfortable and well-lit environment in which to conduct their duties. A fine and laudable sentiment, but how could this apply to all railway premises and in particular the various running sheds? The short answer is that it could not, and there was an exception in the legislation specifically excepting engine sheds where quite clearly it was not just impractical but downright impossible to implement it. (We may suspect that the introduction of this legislation was another nail in the coffin towards the rapid elimination of steam, already foreseen as a consequence of the 1955 Modernisation Plan.) Even so, there were some attempts to improve matters where possible and in particular with regard to lighting. In this (undated) view, the official photographer has recorded a night scene at Stewarts Lane, obviously using time exposure; the normal gloom of the steam shed is seemingly reasonably well lit although it will be noted that there is no obvious sign of movement. (Perhaps everyone had been asked to keep away for a time – they would certainly not miss the opportunity for a 'brew'.)

Above: We now move outside and things are a little different. The point of interest here is not just the engines – Nos 30795 and 34102 will be noted – but in particular the passage of the railwayman with his lamp.

Right: In the third view we are fully outside and can follow the progress of the fitter/fireman whose outline may just be made out on the trestle alongside the engine where he is attending to something under the casing. On the extreme right the horizontal white line may well be associated with the previous filling of the tender on this Bulleid. These three views are undated but are certainly pre-1963. With thanks to Steve Godden.

Above: **Daytime at 'The Lane': the picture features all shapes, sizes and types of locomotive, but is included here because it shows brand-new electric locos Nos E5000 and E5002 (the photographs arrived just too late for inclusion in the special issue on 100 years of the Third Rail). Again undated, it is circa 1958.**

Right: **It would be wonderful to know who these two men are and what they were thinking –any offers? They are possibly both Loco (should we say Traction?) Inspectors in typical railway-issue serge with the new No E5002 in the background.**

Bob Winkworth has kindly submitted these two views of Eastleigh, which show something rather interesting… At first glance this may be taken as a group of workmen from years ago, but it is in fact the building of Campbell Road bridge at Eastleigh, with the houses of Southampton Road on the extreme left. The view is undated but is probably from around the time that the locomotive works moved to Eastleigh and the running shed was built, so circa 1903. Look more closely and there is a view of the original Eastleigh shed in the background. This was located on what later became the access and exit lines to the shed, the point of reference being the signal gantry carrying the arms for the up main home signals and reading (l to r) 'Up main to Salisbury Loop' (at the time the latter was Eastleigh Platform 1); 'Up main to Up Platform' (at the time Platform 2); 'Up main crossover'; and 'Up main through'. The position of the arms and posts should be noted and recalled – because…

…in this next view we have exactly the same gantry, and where the original shed had stood are instead the two lines referred to, with two engines on the left awaiting exit from the shed and a Drummond 4-6-0 coupled to an Adams 4-4-0 arriving on shed. We have never seen a view of the original shed before, once a sub-shed of the main depot at Northam, both of which closed when Eastleigh opened.

The Southern Way

The regular volume for the Southern devotee

BACK ISSUES

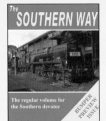

  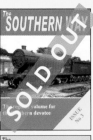  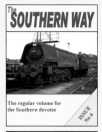

 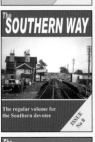   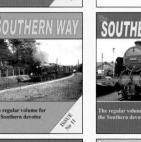

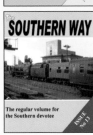 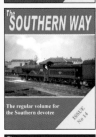  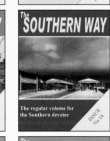 

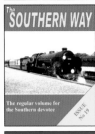   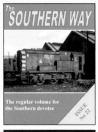 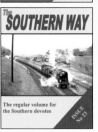 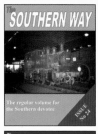

 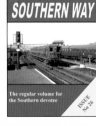   

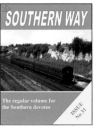 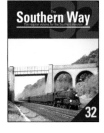

The Southern Way is available from all good book sellers, or in case of difficulty, direct from the publisher. (Post free UK) Each regular issue contains at least 96 pages including colour content.

£11.95 each
£12.95 from Issue 7
£14.50 from Issue 21

Subscription for four-issues available, please see **www.crecy.co.uk** for details. (Post free in the UK)